The Will to Learn

To the Teacher
who loves all children:
now; then; always.

The Will to Learn

Cultivating Student Motivation Without Losing Your Own

Dave Stuart Jr.

FOR INFORMATION:

Corwin

A SAGE Company

2455 Teller Road

Thousand Oaks, California 91320

(800) 233-9936

www.corwin.com

SAGE Publications Ltd.

1 Oliver's Yard

55 City Road

London EC1Y 1SP

United Kingdom

SAGE Publications India Pvt. Ltd.

B 1/I 1 Mohan Cooperative Industrial Area

Mathura Road, New Delhi 110 044

India

SAGE Publications Asia-Pacific Pte. Ltd.

18 Cross Street #10-10/11/12

China Square Central

Singapore 048423

Printed in the United States of America

Library of Congress Control Number: 2023935856

President: Mike Soules

Vice President and
 Editorial Director: Monica Eckman

Executive Editor: Tori Mello Bachman

Content Development Editor: Sharon Wu

Editorial Assistants: Nancy Chung and
 Madison Nevin

Project Editor: Amy Schroller

Copy Editor: Shannon Kelly

Typesetter: C&M Digitals (P) Ltd.

Cover Designer: Gail Buschman

Marketing Manager: Margaret O'Connor

This book is printed on acid-free paper.

23 24 25 26 27 10 9 8 7 6 5 4 3 2 1

Contents

"How do I get there?" is a much easier transaction than "You must go."

—Seth Godin

We inhabit a climate of trust as we inhabit an atmosphere; [we] notice it . . . only when it becomes scarce or polluted.

—Annette Baier

Every day is a learning day.

—Bill Russell

There are only two ways to influence human behavior: you can manipulate it or you can inspire it.

—Simon Sinek

Prologue

Dear colleague,

What you hold in your hand is a book about love. This isn't much of a claim; after all, all good books on teaching come down to studies on love. Love—the active, earnest, and intelligent pursuit of our neighbors' good. Is this not what we spend our labors on each day in our classrooms with our students?

Schools exist for a single purpose: to promote the long-term flourishing of young people. *Specifically,* we do this by teaching them to master disciplines[1] that they likely wouldn't otherwise. The people who do the work of the school—the teachers, the paraprofessionals, the administrators, those who maintain the building, those who serve the food—help human beings become human. Not just some human beings, but every one of them who walks in the door.

In other words, schools are institutions of love—of this earnest seeking and serving of the fullness and wholeness of another. The trouble, of course, is that most of our schools have lost track of this purpose. Most of us still sense its presence, but it's obscured as if by fog. We've lost our grip on what an education *is.* Thankfully, this can change.

* * *

As a university student in Germany in the 1930s, Austrian-born Peter Drucker witnessed the rise of Nazism. He watched as

---

[1] Whenever I say *disciplines* in this book, I mean everything taught in our secondary schools. There are the classic academic disciplines—things such as math and literature and science and social studies. There are the artistic disciplines—things such as painting and drawing and sculpture and theater and music. And there are the "practical" disciplines—things such as home technologies and personal finance and computer applications and construction. In short, we all teach disciplines—ways of seeing, ways of being in the world—and they are all *good, weighty,* and *important.*

institutions—schools, hospitals, government bureaus, churches—became simultaneously *more* productive and *less* humane. The Nazi machine produced one of the most efficiently mobilized populations the world had ever seen—the productivity of its institutions was unmatched—and yet at its root humanity went missing. Nazism transformed institutions into hideous creatures bent on results and power.

So Drucker, who became one of the most influential management thinkers of the twentieth century, was obsessed his entire life with a simple, deep, beautiful question: How do we help institutions become both more productive *and* more humane? This, to me, is the fundamental question that almost no American schools are asking. We see instead two separate emphases.

On the one hand, we want schools to be more productive. Much talk and energy are spent on student achievement, standardized assessment, teacher evaluation, and the science of learning. On the other hand, we want schools to be more humane. Much talk and energy are spent on social-emotional learning, whole-child approaches, teacher work–life balance, self-care, and mental health.

But you *can't* pick just one or the other. To make a school, you must pursue both. The wise practitioner operates in that tiny slice at the center of the productive–humane diagram. In this book I'll share a theory for student motivation that enables our schools to strike this balance.

Striking Drucker's Balance:
An Imperative for Our Schools

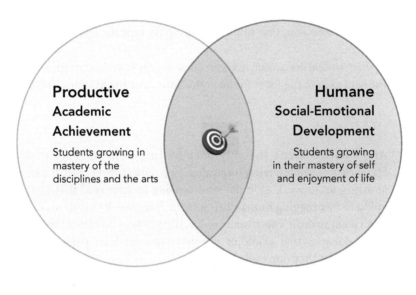

Productive

Academic

Achievement

Students growing in
mastery of the
disciplines and the arts

Humane

Social-Emotional

Development

Students growing
in their mastery of self
and enjoyment of life

* * *

I don't think we have a very good *internal* picture of what demotivation
in a student is like. We've got a great *external* picture of it—head laid
on arms on the desk; dull, affectless eyes; broken record renditions of
"I forgot" and "Do we haaaaaaaave to do this?" We know apathy well.
And yet we're remarkably numb to how apathy *feels* in the heart of a
human being.

Something that helps this, rather quickly, is the following exercise.
Picture how you feel during a terrible professional development
meeting day. I'm talking *terrible*, as in

- the presenter is incompetent or callous;
- the topic is detached from your work as a teacher;
- it's unclear how to even work toward or succeed at what the
  presenter is saying; and
- the presenter is focused on kinds of work that you are
  decidedly *not* a part of.

You can picture that, right? We've all experienced this kind of thing. So now imagine doing that *two* days in a row. Now imagine it three days. Five days. Ten working days. In a row. Of that kind of experience. This is what many of our secondary students experience *every day of the school year*. One hundred and eighty repeats. Day after day.

In short, student demotivation is experienced as pain. It exerts a pressure on the soul akin to the force found at the bottom of the Mariana Trench.

* * *

And students aren't the only ones hurting from this, are they? *Student demotivation is one of the greatest drains on a teacher's spirit.* It's *hard* showing up to work each day and sensing in your soul that you're going to be dragging human beings into doing work that they really don't want to do. It's spiritually exhausting to lean on carrot-or-stick methodologies that cajole or coerce young-yet-total persons into doing things they don't want to do.

In response to this pain, we are reduced to a kind of professional thrashing about. We resort to complex grading systems, faddish pedagogies, "fix my problem" purchases on Teachers Pay Teachers. We complain; we become despondent. In all these reactions, we're like a patient in the hospital who mashes the bedside button for a fresh infusion of pain meds. Once in awhile, we can get the pain to go away, but the *problem's* not leaving.

* * *

What's bizarre about all of this is something fundamental to young human beings in the twenty-first century: *You've never met a student who set out to become demotivated in school.* Every one of your students, down in the roots of their wills, *desires* to desire to learn.

That word *desire* is important to contemplate. It comes from the Latin *desirare*, with *de* connoting "from within, deep down," and *sidere* meaning "from the stars." That's a weird word, right? Etymologists surmise that originally the verb meant something like "to await what the stars will bring."

Let the word's beauty sink in.

Then look out on your classroom and see, deep in those eyes looking back, an unyielding *desire*—an awaiting of what the stars will bring.

* * *

So what's the vision of this book? What am I aiming at for us—me here in my classroom in western Michigan, you there in your classroom in your part of the world? What will this book *practically* allow you and me to know and do?

To answer generally, my writing here aims at what it always does: to help us promote the long-term flourishing of young people without sacrificing our lives on the altars of professional success. I'm a *both-and* kind of guy. I believe being a *great teacher* requires cultivating a *great life*. You can't do one without the other. And to do both of those things, you've got to have time and space to think and practice and grow and sustain.

To answer for this book particularly, this volume contains the best ideas I've learned about creating the conditions that help students *want* to do the work of learning—the conditions that help them *genuinely care* to learn. It is an in-depth extension of ideas I began exploring in the second chapter of *These 6 Things: How to Focus Your Teaching on What Matters Most*. This book is that book's sequel.

Toward that end, I want to help you and me partner with reality by realizing

- that every one of our students *wants* to want to learn,

- that every instance of student demotivation is experienced as pain,

- that every school in the world can be both productive *and* humane—achievement and wellness aren't opposed to one another but instead are friends,

- that you and I have an outlandish (but not omnipotent) influence on the degree to which students in our classrooms experience the will to learn, and
- that the most powerful strategies for cultivating student motivation are far from complicated.

Partnership with reality—that is what we're after.

* * *

So, dear colleague, are you ready? Then let's put on our gardening gloves and begin.

Teaching right beside you,

DSJR

April 2023

CHAPTER 1

On the Teaching of Souls Toward Long-Term Flourishing

The trouble with students is that they're invisible.

Not entirely, of course. I can see my students' faces and hairs and fingers and pencils and clothes. Obviously. The trouble is just that these things are such a small percentage of what students *are*.

I can't see, for example, how hungry a student is, or how the food they ate last night is affecting their biochemistry, or whether their body was adequately restored last night via quality REM and NREM cycles. I can't see whether a student's mind and chest are tight with anxiety or weighed down by depression. I can't see the status of a certain student's relationship with her mother, her father, her siblings, her friends. I can't see a student's latest flights of mental fancy, the things that secretly thrill or bother him, the deep, inchoate hopes he has for the fullness of his existence. I can't see what a student learned last year—about my subject, about school, about what it means to learn. And this is true for every student on every roster I teach.

See what I mean? They're invisible creatures. And that's troublesome!

So, our first task in this book is getting down to the roots of our students' hearts, down to the very bottom of the most powerful part of each human being, down into the mostly forgotten world of the human will. What you and I are going to try to do, colleague, is nothing less than impact that place, that center, that heart, in each of our students, using strategies that on their face will seem laughably simple.

That's this book.

It's not about willpower in the brain—we'll talk very little about that fine organ here as there are plenty of folks better qualified to discuss such things with you. We're after volition in the heart, in the very spirit. We're after the genuine, thriving, bright will to learn and how to create the kinds of schools and classrooms that align with the realities of the human heart.

A Creature of Five Parts

So here's the deal: I think it makes greatest sense to think of our students as beings comprised of five interrelated parts. And don't give me credit for this model—that goes to a late University of Southern California phenomenologist philosopher named Dallas Willard.

Basically, Willard argued, human beings have five parts:

- the intellectual part—that is, our thoughts;
- the emotional part—our feelings;

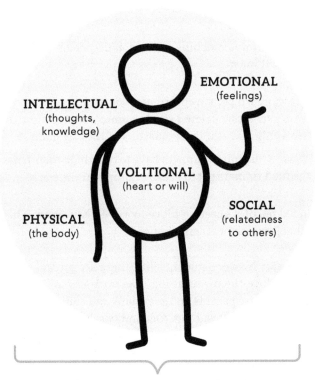

we make more sense when you think of us as five-part creatures

- the physical part—our bodies;
- the social part—our relations with others; and
- the volitional part—our will, our heart, our executive center, the part of us that initiates and creates.

The interwoven whole of these five parts is called, in Willard's parlance, a soul. This is an old-fashioned, multicultural concept that aligns with the invisibleness that we touched on a moment ago. As much as you and I and our students are bodies, we're also minds and intentions and relationships. The long-term flourishing of a human being, then, depends on development in all of these aspects of the soul.

Which starts to get us to the work you and I do as teachers. What's this soul stuff got to do with school?

Know Thy Lane

Some time ago, I was watching a 400m, four-person relay. I noticed two beautiful things:

1. The way each person contributes something critical to the team's success—delete a single runner's contribution and the team only makes it three-quarters of the way home.
2. The way the initial runners have to remain in their lanes but the final runners get to use the fullness of the track.

It reminded me of a question I love to ask: In education, what's our lane? What is our critical contribution?

Here's my take: In every student's life, there are myriad adults who in some way love them—meaning, *who work for their good, who will their good.*[1] There are parents and guardians and aunts and uncles and neighbors and pastors and mentors and coaches and troop leaders and event organizers and teachers . . . just all kinds of people who seek, in ways big or small, to develop young people. You can add in all the caveats you'd like—and I'll grant you there are plenty—but the zoomed-out picture is that the promotion of a child's long-term flourishing *isn't just up to us.*[2]

In short, *long-term flourishing is a group project.*

So, what role do schools uniquely play in this project?

We develop the mind by helping students to grow in mastery of the disciplines and the arts.

Yep, our job is the head.

---

[1] Willard (2002) defined love as "the genuine inner readiness and longing to secure someone's good" (p. 24).

[2] And woe to us when in hubris we forget this!

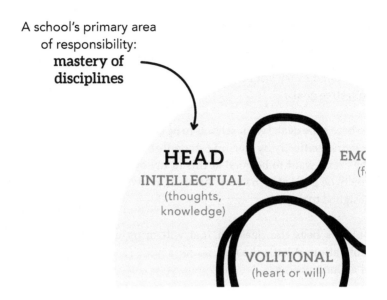

A school's primary area
of responsibility:
**mastery of
disciplines**

HEAD
INTELLECTUAL
(thoughts,
knowledge)

EMC
(f

VOLITIONAL
(heart or will)

Now, I'm not giving license here to ignore socio-emotional learning (SEL)—by all means, we ought to seek the social and the emotional and the physical development of young people in our schools. Yes, sign me up. Sign all of us up—just a skim of our culture is enough to see how dire are the costs of widespread social and emotional immaturity.

But look: The *intellect* is our lane. If we miss it, we sabotage the relay race.

Consider this:

- Plenty of people in students' lives will seek to teach them healthy conflict resolution—an aspect of social learning—yet who else will teach them literature or history like you do?
- All sorts of folks will contribute to a child's understanding of how to process difficult emotions—a key outcome of emotional learning—but how many will make it their mission to teach health or physics or physical education or geometry?

Now come on, Dave, you may be thinking. *Life's not all about the head!*

Of course it isn't! And a 4x400 relay isn't all about the second lap. Nonetheless, the second runner must be humble enough to run their component of the race, striving for excellence in it alone, seeking to eke from it every last bit of performance they can for the sake of the collective goal.

So here's the deal: I want schools to be good at the development of the mind, specifically by teaching students to master the disciplines and the arts. I want to be good at this in my own classroom, and I want you to be good at it in yours. After all, it's what schools are uniquely designed to do.

But this begs the question that will bring us, finally, to student motivation: What's the best power source for developing the mind of a human being?

The Two Ingredients in Mastering Anything

In order for a person to get better at something—for example, writing a report in biology, or playing a note on the flute, or lengthening a long jump, or developing lines of code in computer science class—at least two basic things have to happen. The person doing the growing must

1. do work, and

2. do it with care.

In most conversations I have with teachers, concern rests primarily on the first part: getting students to do work. While researching this book, I catalogued too many systems and methods that have been developed for getting students to do work, the most popular of which amount to carrot-stick combos.

- Carrots incentivize the doing of work. Get on the honor roll. Become valedictorian. Get into a good college. Get scholarships.

- Sticks consequentialize the *not doing* of work. Get mandatory study hall. Get a phone call home. Miss getting into college. Miss a scholarship. Get placed on academic probation from the team.

Both of these rely on a simple principle about people: *It's possible, through punishment or reward, to coerce behavior.*

But here is the more critical principle: *You cannot coerce care.*

A person who does a thing—who even does it well—is not necessarily a person who cares about what they've done. Instead, the person can be driven by care for the carrots or the sticks. This, I would argue, is the condition of most folks who do well in our secondary schools today: They want the stuff that educational success *gets them*—the degree, the salary, the job—while not being all that interested in *the education itself.*

What I'd like to put forth in this book is that a such a person, regardless of grades or achievement, is actually a poorly motivated human soul. They'll do work, but it won't be done from the fullness of their agency. And so, eventually, they'll find themselves alienated from the fundamental goodness of learning. They'll lose the sensory capacity for tasting and seeing that an education is *good.*

And, counterintuitively, removing carrots or sticks from schools doesn't seem to optimally solve this big problem. In my view, getting rid of all consequences and/or all incentives doesn't magically grow care. You can't subtract your way to a solution here.

The good news is that I've seen teachers in all kinds of systems—including those rife with carrots or sticks—cultivate a deep care for learning in their classrooms.

Before we move on, let me explicitly say that when we rely on carrot and stick combos to get students to do work, we shouldn't be surprised to see middling returns on all that hard work. At the end of the day, you just can't arrive at mastery without *care.*

What's Care Got to Do With Mastery?

In all the literature on expertise development (i.e., mastery and its pursuit), there's a term you'll see more than any other: *deliberate practice.*

The late K. Anders Ericsson spent his career studying the development of expertise, but his breakthrough discovery came in the first couple years of his work. In one of his earliest studies, Ericsson found that, through a certain kind of practice over the course of two years, a guy that he was working with went from being able to memorize eight random digits read aloud to memorizing eighty-two.[3]

Eighty. Freaking. Two![4]

This shattered records from previous studies.

Then Ericsson started looking at other fields where records were being or had been shattered, and he began noticing a pattern: These new levels of mastery were the fruit of a certain *kind* of work. He called this work *deliberate practice*, and by now this is a term many of us educators have heard of.

Deliberate practice involves these steps:

1. Identify a specific subskill that incrementally challenges you.
2. Practice that skill with full effort.
3. Seek feedback on what you could do better.[5]

As I recorded that three-part description, I had a bit of an epiphany. Deliberate practice is something I want my students to do, but it's not something that I spend any time at all talking to them about or teaching them. In my own classroom practice with ninth-grade students in a small midwestern town, it's just not a thing I've spoken much about with my students.[6]

---

[3]That's a number that looks like this: 10498273756472830192847585427384920 394758693021948573698502345091827450189734456823.

[4]Ericcson tells this story in the first pages of *Peak: Secrets from the New Science of Expertise* (2016).

[5]This language comes from Character Lab's explainer page on the concept.

[6]Now, as we'll see in Strategy 7, I *do* take great care to teach my students how to work hard and smart. But, if you were to ask my students, "What does deliberate practice mean?" none of them would be able to answer you because of anything I had taught them.

This is because I am interested in a more fundamental problem: How in the world do I help classes filed with diverse students to *care enough* about the work of learning to do things such as identify subskills, put forth full effort, and seek feedback for improvement?

This, to me, has far greater leverage than teaching secondary students something as abstract as deliberate practice. And *that's* because beneath deliberate practice, beneath the kind of work that optimally advances mastery, is *care*, is the *enlisted will*, is the *signed-up volitional core of our students' souls.*

Care is to potential energy in the classroom as the sun is to potential energy on the earth. There's no force in your classroom more laden with power than care.

A Beliefs-Based Methodology for Motivation in the Classroom (Or: What's at the Root of Care?)

A school's primary area
of responsibility:
**students mastering
disciplines (the head)**

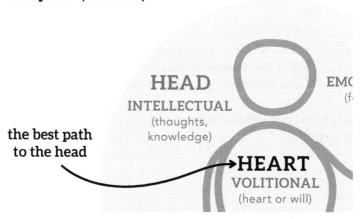

**the best path
to the head**

HEAD
INTELLECTUAL
(thoughts,
knowledge)

EMC
(f

HEART
VOLITIONAL
(heart or will)

As an educator, you've likely heard about intrinsic motivation. Usually, what we mean by this is a summary of Richard Ryan and Edward Deci's Self-Determination Theory. An easy way to understand Ryan and Deci is provided by popularizer Pink (2009) in his book *Drive: The Surprising Truth About What Motivates Us*. In the book, Pink summarizes motivation as consisting of three factors: autonomy, mastery, and purpose. When a person experiences these factors, that person will tend to care about the work they are doing. This is Self-Determination Theory in a nutshell.

My trouble with Ryan and Deci has always been, however, that the model for education they describe seems so far removed from the realities of my classroom. The realities of my job place constraints on what I can do with my curriculum, on how my students' days are scheduled, on what my students have experienced in school leading up to their ninth-grade year with me, and on what they'll experience afterward.

It's not that Self-Determination Theory isn't great, it's just that it's not nearly as useful to my classroom practice as the what I call the Five Key Beliefs. So, I'm no psychologist, but for what it's worth I'd like to offer our profession the Five Key Beliefs Theory. If we get good at cultivating these five key things in the hearts of our students, I think all kinds of schools can make better on their promise to advance all students toward mastery. All kinds of schools can be better places to learn and work. This theory can work in places with all kinds of curricula, all kinds of constraints or freedoms, all kinds of cultures, all kinds of demographic formulations.

So, the Five Key Beliefs. Yes. These are what I see all across the literature, both within and outside of education; these cry out to me in every one of my classrooms and all the ones I visit. It's a simple but powerful idea: at the root of care are beliefs.[7]

Beliefs fuel care-driven behavior. And it's not just any beliefs. It's five in particular.

---

[7]What's a belief? We'll get deep into this question in Chapter 2. In brief, however, belief is knowledge held in the will; it's an effortless confidence in a thing. It's a certainty, a trust; it's a readiness to act as if something were true (that last one is Dallas Willard). From what we believe, we assume. Beliefs are so deeply rooted that you'll know them more by what people do rather than what they say they think.

CREDIBILITY	My teacher knows what she's doing. He's good at his job. He cares about this work. She can help me grow. He can take me to the next level. I'm fortunate to be in this class with this teacher.
VALUE	This work matters to me. It's interesting. It's useful. It's beautiful. It's meaningful. I can use it to help others. I won't regret giving this my time and energy. This isn't a waste of time.
EFFORT	If I apply myself, I can get better at this. I can grow in my knowledge. I can make myself smarter. I've not arrived yet; I'm still in the beginning stages, and that's neat.
EFFICACY	I can succeed at this. I know what success looks like, and I can get there—it's possible for me. I'm on the right track.
BELONGING	People like me do work like this. I fit here—in this place, in this moment, with these people, in this work.

These Five Key Beliefs are at the root of student motivation.[8] They explain why markedly different-looking classrooms can have such similar motivational dynamics. What I mean is, let's say you were to find me a dozen classrooms sprinkled throughout the world. In each of these classrooms, students do work with care and are growing in mastery, but that's *all* they have in common. Otherwise, they're completely different—different pedagogies, different physical spaces, different subjects, different student ability levels, different demographics, different teacher personalities.

Sounds a bit chaotic, right? But at the root of all of these places you'll see the same thing again and again: thousands of contextual signals pointing student hearts toward the Five Key Beliefs.

When the heart is all set, the mind is primed for development. And understanding the Five Key Beliefs can help you get the heart set in *all kinds of settings*.

The Five Key Beliefs, in other words, pave the path to the head.

Because the path to the head, it turns out, is through the heart.

---

[8]You'll often see these beliefs written about as *mindsets*. I don't like that term because it muddies the distinct difference that I see between the mind and the will. Even researchers seem to struggle with this distinction; when they define the term *mindset* in their books and papers, they almost always use the word *belief*. But belief is a remarkably muddy concept in Western culture. In the next chapter, we'll filter out the mud.

CHAPTER 2

The Five Key Beliefs
How They Work

Belief is one of my favorite words in the English language. I root for it. It is a conceptual diamond in a rough of words that mean little. But belief is widely misunderstood.

Many mistake belief as mere intellectual agreement. But in this book we're using a more fundamental definition of *belief*—belief as trust, as certainty, as something known at a level much deeper than the head.

In this chapter, I'd like to lay out five key qualities useful in understanding the Five Key Beliefs that we're specifically focused on in this book. It may be tempting to skip this chapter, but please don't! What you're after is becoming the kind of professional who sees and understands the Five Key Beliefs layer of your classroom. To do that, you need the ideas that we'll now explore.

Quality 1: The Five Key Beliefs Are Knowledge Held in the Will.

pexels.com/Thirdman

This isn't something people ponder, is it? And that's because we just trust chairs. They have always worked for us. Apart from the one time in grade school when a mischievous pal pulled a chair out from behind me, I've always known chairs to function in ways I can rely upon. And as a result, guess what? I believe deeply in chairs. I *know* that they work, not just in my mind but in my heart, my will.

And so, in an age of strident polarization, behold: Chairs are a belief that unites us all.

- We sit in them all the time.

- We trust them—even ones we've never sat in.

- Our friends all sit in them.

Now that's all pretty mundane, isn't it? But that's part of my point.

Belief is *mundane*. It's the stuff of the everyday—the stuff you don't even think about. Instead, you just *know* it, and you act on it, and you do so again and again and again and again, without thinking.

Belief is the bedrock of assumption. And from this foundation, we enact our lives.

Or, in other words, belief is knowledge you hold in your will. That's what we're after in cultivating the Five Key Beliefs in our students. We want Credibility and Value and Belonging and Effort and Efficacy to be nonchalant assumptions. We want the Five Key Beliefs to become as obvious in our classrooms as the presence of air.

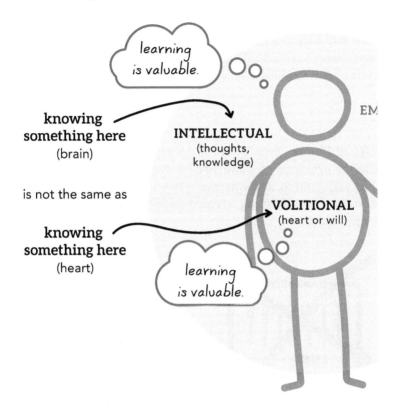

Belief is knowledge held in the will. It's an effortless confidence in a thing. It's a certainty, a trust. It's a readiness to act as if something were true (that's how Dallas Willard explained it). It's largely invisible, as much to us as it is to others. Through our beliefs, we see and interpret the world.

Why It's Important to Know This in a Classroom

If you think a belief is something you can just get a student to articulate to you, you'll be really confused when student actions don't align with what they've said. For example, early in my research I remember teaching students about growth mindset, and we even reached a point where virtually all of them "had" a growth mindset, according to a questionnaire we took in class. There was just one problem: My students were still afraid of failure, still acted helpless when they got stuck, still were quick to quit when things got hard. They had what Carol Dweck has since labelled *false growth mindset*.[1] And this trouble, it turned out, stemmed from my misunderstanding regarding belief.

Try This

Think of Five Key Beliefs work as the cultivation of a garden rather than the operation of a switchboard. Our students' hearts are not filled with buttons and switches—*Okay, let's turn on some Credibility, let's switch on some Belonging, let's crank the dial on Effort*—but instead are complex gardens.

iconfinder.com/Chatnut is Industries; iconfinder.com/Lucian Dinu

I like the garden picture better because it implies the key verb in creating a care-driven classroom: *cultivate*. This word is marvelous for conceptualizing how motivation works in a classroom. It denotes preparing lands for a crop and can also be used in the sense of human relationships (e.g., "He sought to cultivate an image as a fair teacher," or "She sought to cultivate a strong relationship with all her students"). In all of its uses, however, the word *cultivate* describes a partnership: There are things that the cultivator intends and enacts, but there are also things that the cultivator does not control. The land has its own agency. One's image depends on the perceptions of others. A relationship takes two.

This is so unlike the switchboard, isn't it? The switchboard is under the complete control of the one pushing the buttons and moving the

---

[1]See page 168 for more on this idea of false growth mindset.

slides. The garden, on the other hand, is a living thing. It requires partnership. It cannot be omnipotently run.

And this is how student motivation works, too. It's so obvious when we read it on a page like this one, but just think of how many times our frustrations in this job seem founded, when we're honest, on the unrealistic idea that our students ought to act a bit more like switchboards.

There's a lot more work to cultivating a garden than running a switchboard. Many actions are involved in cultivation: planning, prepping the soil, planting seeds, watering, fertilizing, weeding, pruning, picking. This is also how it works with student motivation. Work is required. Yet it's possible to master the art of cultivating student motivation just as it's possible to master the art of gardening. The work is complex, but at the same time it is knowable. Through practice and study, we can gain a reliable competence in this area.

Finally, when a garden is properly stewarded and when its management is seen as a partnership with reality and as a craft to be mastered . . . wow, can it ever be rewarding!

This is all to say that there's a critical conceptual shift that we here must make: The hearts of our students are gardens, not switchboards.

Quality 2: All of the Five Key Beliefs Exist on a Spectrum in the Heart of Every One of Your Students.

Actually, I'm serious. I really don't know about chairs anymore.

pexels.com/Thirdman

All right, let's go back to chairs. Let's imagine that I did a bad experiment on you, and for each of the next seven days I sabotaged three or four chairs I knew you were going to sit on. Every time you sat in one of my sabotaged chairs, it failed spectacularly. By the end of the week, you've had two dozen chairs collapse beneath you; you've been humiliated and are physically sore.

Following this experiment, would you think twice about sitting in chairs? Absolutely you would. Because *I would have moved your belief in chairs into the realm of questioning and fear.*

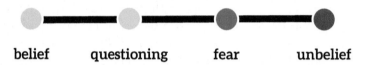

belief   questioning   fear   unbelief

Now, let's consider a student in our classroom—we'll call him Johnny Johnson. First week of school, I'm super nice to him and super passionate about where we're going as learners this year. I learn his name real quick, maybe even make a quick positive phone call home. I'm clear, calm, and warmly authoritative.[2] That's probably plenty of signals for Johnny to believe that I'm a good teacher. He probably thinks, "Mr. Stuart's got what it takes to help me learn this year."

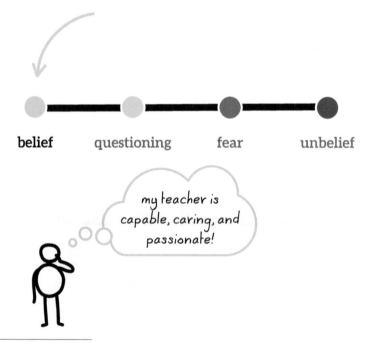

---

[2]We'll discuss warmly authoritative teacher presence more on page 82.

But then in October I snip at one of Johnny's friends for interrupting me. I take three weeks to give feedback on a set of student essays. My warm-up isn't posted before class starts a few days in a row (see Strategy 3 on page 91).

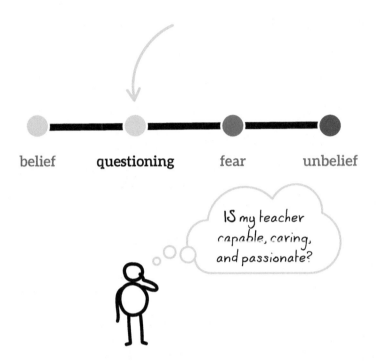

(By the way, if you're starting to feel bad about yourself, take heart. All of these examples are picked from my own career. I'll get to some good news in a minute. But first, the pit must deepen.)

In November, things don't get better. I assign Johnny's class an essay that feels pretty last minute, muttering something like, "Well, we just have to get it done by Friday. Department deadline. Do your best." It ends up being a confusing assignment, and when Johnny and over half his classmates raise their hands at the same time, I snap, "Listen, just get started on your introduction, and I'll be around to help as many as I can." Unfortunately, the bell rings before I get to Johnny.

When Johnny finally gets the essay back from me a few weeks later, he sees that he's gotten an A. The thing is, *he doesn't understand why*. He's not even sure I read it.

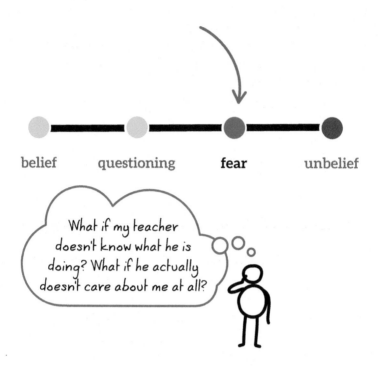

Keep in mind that these aren't things Johnny is necessarily conscious of. Remember, belief is knowledge held in the will, not the head. Johnny's heart is shifting in response to the signals he's getting in the context of my classroom, signals that increasingly indicate that I don't know what I'm doing or that I don't care about him.

Things still don't improve. By January, Johnny's developed a good grade in the class, but he's not really proud of it. Writing is a grind for him; he just puts things on paper and hopes the grade turns out all right. Because after all, that's what the class is—it's a grade, a credit toward graduation, just something to get through. Even Mr. Stuart basically tells him that.

For the first few minutes of each class period, there's nothing for Johnny and his peers to do. They talk, goof off, check their phones. Mr. Stuart, meanwhile, "takes attendance" on a website that looks a lot like his e-mail. When he's finally ready, Mr. Stuart has to yell over the class to get them to quiet down. While he's explaining the day's agenda, Johnny heckles him a few times, and Mr. Stuart laughs. Johnny has a fine relationship with Mr. Stuart. I mean, c'mon, Mr. Stuart's a cool guy.

He's just not a very good teacher, that's all.

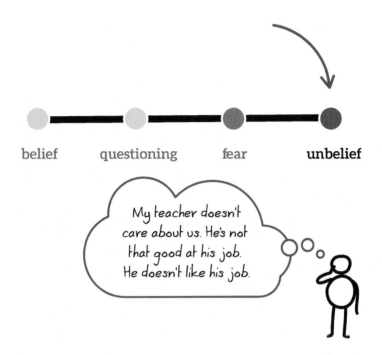

Wow Dave, that was super depressing!

Right!? I even got myself sad writing that.

The good news is that the spectrum can go the opposite way, too, and *that's* the kind of movement this book hopes to incite. I've seen it happen hundreds of times, and you likely have too. I just thought the depressing story would lend some needed gravitas to all the stick-figure pictures, you know?

To Put It Briefly

The Five Key Beliefs all exist on a spectrum. The heart of every student in your classroom and school can be found somewhere in the rows of the following grid.

	BELIEF	QUESTIONING	FEAR	UNBELIEF
CREDIBILITY	My teacher is capable, caring, and passionate.	Is my teacher capable, caring, and passionate?	What if my teacher doesn't care? What if my teacher is incompetent?	My teacher is not capable, caring, and passionate.
VALUE	My work matters. It means something. It'll help me.	Does my work matter? Will it help me? Is there meaning here?	What if this work is pointless? What if I'm wasting my time?	My work is pointless. It is a waste of time. This class is dumb. No one cares.
EFFORT	I know the kind of Effort that pays off. If I put that Effort in, I'll become better and stronger.	Gosh, I'm working hard. Is this going to pay off?	What if no matter how hard I try, I don't improve? What if some people have it, but I don't?	I've seen that Effort doesn't pay off here. It's talent that matters. No matter how hard I try, I won't get better. I'm as good as I can get.
EFFICACY	I can succeed at this.	Can I succeed at this?	What if I fail?	I can't succeed at this. No matter what I do, I'll fail.
BELONGING	I fit here. My struggles are normal. People like me do work like this.	Do I fit here? Am I the only one struggling?	Do these people know how badly I fit in? Do they realize how below-the-norm my abilities are?	I don't fit here. My struggles are unique to me. People with my identity don't do work like this.

Why It's Important to Know This in a Classroom

It's common for teachers to say things like, "Well, that student is just not motivated." The spectrum idea teaches us that it's not that simple, which is really good news. It's more accurate to say, "At present, the student doesn't seem to believe

- that math matters (Value)," or
- that she can improve her understanding of science (Effort)," or
- that Ms. Smith is a good computer science teacher (Credibility)."

This is what I mean when I say that the Five Key Beliefs methodology can help us analyze student motivation puzzles with far greater effectiveness than we currently tend to do. Accurate analysis enables effective action.

Try This

Think of Five Key Beliefs work as the alleviation of fear more than the indoctrination of thought. Remember, you're after knowledge in the will, not knowledge in the head. Fear is situated not in the head as much as it is in the will; despite our knowledge and logic, snakes or mice or spiders or heights or sharks still creep us out. This view helps you to feel empowered when you encounter demotivation in your setting.

Quality 3: The Five Key Beliefs Are Hierarchically Interrelated

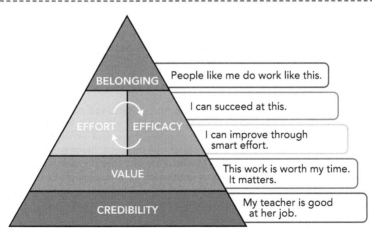

In this section, let's let a picture be worth a thousand words. The image above shows how the beliefs relate to one another in a classroom that is focused on student mastery.[3] This simple, childish-looking diagram took me years to develop. In my daily classroom practice, it guides me. In my work with educators round the world, it's like the GPS in our phones.

To get the diagram's full value, I need you to pretend you're building a pyramid with a child's blocks, with it being impossible to build the second layer (in our case, Value) without first building the first (for us, Credibility). It took me several years of classroom practice to realize this hierarchy in the Five Key Beliefs, and seeing the hierarchy makes it much easier for overwhelmed teachers to prioritize.

Let me explain. Let's say that you're a newer teacher who is not used to this Five Key Beliefs way of approaching student motivation. You want things to be better in your classroom motivationally—for both your sake and your students'—but when you look at all Five Key Beliefs you get overwhelmed.

Before understanding the hierarchy of the beliefs, I didn't know what to tell a teacher like this. But now it's obvious: Focus on the Credibility belief. A noncredible teacher will find it exceptionally difficult to help students to value the work of learning in their class. Students may value the work of learning in the class anyway, but in this case it will be *despite* the teacher, not because of the teacher.

But when a teacher is credible—that is, when a student believes that the teacher is good at their job, cares, and knows what they are doing, and that the teacher's work matters to them—then that teacher can start influencing the Value belief just by regularly and creatively speaking to the value of the work of learning in their class (which is what Strategy 4's winsome and sure apologetics are all about).[4]

Because Credibility is so foundational to the Five Key Beliefs methodology, focus on it before you move on to Value. If I can only aid you in mastering the cultivation of one of the key beliefs, I want it to be Credibility.

---

[3]It is really important to note that this diagram is limited to classrooms focused on mastery. If your classroom is focused on other elements of the student soul—say, the social element, or the emotional element—then the power dynamics within the Five Key Beliefs might be different. Belonging might be most important in such a setting. Maybe. I am not sure because my work is focused on promoting the long-term flourishing of young people by teaching them to master the disciplines and the arts. When I treat social and emotional learning, it's a side mission, not the main mission.

[4]See page 123 for discussion of this.

And, if I can only aid you in mastering *two* beliefs, the next would be Value. After all, look at the Effort, Efficacy, and Belonging beliefs described in the Five Key Beliefs pyramid. If a student doesn't think the work of learning in their physical education or physics or computer science class is important—if instead they think it's lame or boring or a waste of time or needlessly frustrating or embarrassing—then why would that student care if they can improve through their efforts, or succeed at tasks, or belong to this group? A student needs to value something in order to be much invested in those subsequent beliefs.

On top of Value we have Effort and Efficacy. For years I couldn't decide which one of these went on top of the other. I saw in the research and in my classroom that each needed the other; in any classroom, a student needs to exert wise, strategic Effort[5] in order to increase the likelihood of good results, and those good results will then drive future Effort and striving. I like to represent this dynamic in what I call the Effort and Efficacy Flywheel; it's from this relationship that we get the circular arrows in the Five Key Beliefs pyramid above.

The Effort-Efficacy Flywheel

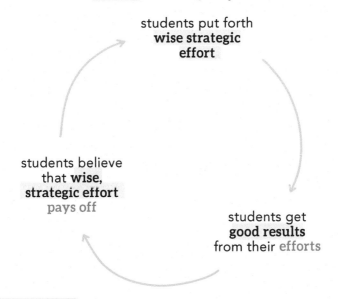

students put forth
**wise strategic
effort**

students get
good results
from their efforts

students believe
that **wise,
strategic effort**
pays off

---

[5]This is so important. I meet many teachers who complain that their students don't have a good work ethic. But one of the core reasons for this lack of observable effort is often that students have not been *taught* by *experts* (i.e., us) *how* to learn effectively.

And finally, Belonging caps it all off. Once the prior four beliefs are well-cultivated, Belonging typically takes care of itself—after all, who wouldn't want to belong to a classroom community where the teacher is credible, the work is valuable, and improvement and success (Effort and Efficacy) are all but assured?

To Put It Briefly

Use the Five Key Beliefs pyramid as your guide to "build from the bottom." Focus first on cultivating Credibility, then Value, then Effort and Efficacy, and finally Belonging. As you go, you'll find your belief cultivation efforts increasingly aided by the foundations you've laid through this progression.

Why It's Important to Know This in a Classroom

The Five Key Beliefs can be overwhelming to a teacher when learning about them for the first time. What I always say is that if you can only focus on one of the beliefs, focus on Credibility. It's especially malleable, it's the most within your control, and it's the point of best leverage from which to influence the other beliefs. Two of its components—care and passion—have strategies you can start tomorrow.[6]

With that said, once you get a handle on all the beliefs, you're going after all of them all the time in the context of the mastery work you're doing with students. This becomes a part of your soul-gardener's green thumb, and you use it seamlessly.

Try This

For a rapid improvement in Credibility no matter where you are in the school year, begin with Strategy 1 on page 47.

Quality 4: The Five Key Beliefs Are Dependent on Context

I don't know if it's possible to overexaggerate four things about the classroom context:

1. how important it is to cultivate student motivation and therefore student mastery,

---

[6]See Strategies 1 and 3 and page 47 and 91, respectively.

2. how complex the classroom context is,

3. how little control we have over it, and

4. how nonetheless *massively powerful* our small slice of control is.

Remember that thing about each of our students being souls—hypercomplex amalgamations of five distinct parts of being? Now multiply that by every person in the class, and then take that and multiply it by every experience any of these people has ever had. That is your classroom's motivational context.

It's kind of like what happened when scientists pointed the Hubble telescope at the same spot in the sky for fifty days in a row. If you held your thumb at arm's length to cover the moon, the patch imaged by the Hubble eXtreme Deep Field was approximately the size of a pinhead.[7]

So what happened? It was crazy. Previously dark portions of sky turned out to be littered with not planets, not stars, but *galaxies*. There were thousands of them. (Image below.)

Image Credit: NASA, ESA, H. Teplitz and M. Rafelski (IPAC/Caltech), A. Koekemoer (STScI), R. Windhorst (Arizona State University), and Z. Levay (STScI)

[7]At the time of this writing, humanity received an even clearer version of this photograph thanks to the James Webb telescope. What a wonderful time to be alive in the cosmos, colleague.

Galaxies have about one hundred billion stars in them apiece. One hundred billion of our suns, multiplied by thousands, multiplied by all the rest of the night sky beyond the pinhead-sized spot Hubble looked at. Some scientists—*scientists*—even go so far as to say that the number of stars in the universe may be infinite. Stupefyingly grandiose is a fair summary of our cosmological context.

And *that's* what the classroom context is like. The more you learn about teaching and people and your discipline and yourself, the more you think, *Oooookay. There is a lot happening here.* And all of this context is influencing student motivation all of the time. Each experience, bias, and attribute of every student individually and of each student in relation to every other student has an effect on the degree to which students find us credible, find the work valuable, find Effort worthwhile, find success possible (Efficacy), or find that they belong in our rooms doing the work of our disciplines.

All the details are in play, all the time. So, faced with such scale, I see two potential responses:

Option 1: "Wow. I'm existentially horrified right now."

or

Option 2: The Five Key Beliefs give us a methodology for finding signal within that noise; we have a lens filter that helps us to see the layer of motivation and intervene intelligently. The Five Key Beliefs help us turn chaos into concept and therein find agency when faced with the difficulty of student demotivation.

To Put It Briefly

The classroom context is complicated, but instead of lamenting this we ought to roll up our sleeves and get to work understanding the parts of it we can best influence. Beliefs are largely context-dependent, *especially* in secondary students. How we shape the school or classroom context is enormously predictive of the degree to which students will pursue mastery with care. And we shape that context every day, during every encounter.

Why It's Important to Know This in a Classroom

You only control so much in a room—a sliver of the total context—but what you *do* control is *massively influential*. Be sure you know the difference between what you do and don't control in your context.[8]

Try This

Think of Five Key Beliefs work as the sending of signals.[9] Amidst the complexity of a classroom, we want to be consistently producing signals—through our words and our actions, our lessons and our assignments, and our policies and procedures—that we're credible, that the work is valuable, that each student belongs here, and that smart Effort can yield growth and success and the success of growth (Efficacy). I like this image of the radio tower because folks who work at radio towers don't control whether or not their signal is received, but they have complete control over whether or not the signal is sent. This must be the teacher's mindset.

Quality 5: The Five Key Beliefs Are Malleable.

Credit: Photo by Brooke Fournier.

[8]I've been told, "But Dave, that stuff I don't control is super important. We've got to fix these massive systemic problems." And hey, I'm probably with you on that. *But* I've yet to find a school where the elements within that school's control are being optimally leveraged for the long-term flourishing of students. For the sake of students in classrooms today, I recommend attending to this riper fruit first.

[9]I owe Coyle (2018) and his book The Culture Code for teaching me this language of signal-sending.

The research is clear: The Five Key Beliefs move. They can shift in a week, in a month, in a year. They can shift *for* a week, a month, a year. A student can go from demotivated in science class in September to scheduling elective science classes in February. A student can think you're the worst teacher ever and after a five-minute conversation be back to finding you credible.

This doesn't mean students are fickle; it means people are. And that's not a knock on us, either—gardens are fickle, too, right? And beautiful. And filled with life. And good.

Let me share a study by Miu and Yeager (2014) that explores this.

THE STUDY

Six hundred freshmen students from three different high schools were given a short reading and writing exercise in September of their ninth-grade year. They were randomly assigned to an intervention group (Group A) or a control group (Group B) without knowing which group they were in.

According to a press release about the study,

> Students assigned to [Group A] read a passage describing how individuals' personalities are subject to change. The passage emphasized that being bullied is not the result of a fixed, personal deficiency, nor are bullies essentially "bad" people. An article about brain plasticity and endorsements from older students accompanied the passage. After reading the materials, the students were asked to write their own narrative about how personalities can change, to be shared with future ninth graders.

> Students in [Group B] read a passage that focused on the malleability of a trait not related to personality: athletic ability.

In other words, kids read a passage, an article, and some words from older students, and then they wrote a narrative summarizing what they had learned. For one group, the readings were about how personality can change and social exclusion isn't permanent; for the other group, the readings were about how athletic ability can change. The exercise took up a class period.

From the press release (emphasis mine):

> A follow-up 9 months later in May showed that rates of clinically significant depressive symptoms rose by roughly 39% among students in [Group B], in line with previous research on depression in adolescence. [In other words, Group B's activity neither harmed nor benefited the students.]

> Students [in Group A] who learned about the malleability of personality, on the other hand, showed *no such increase in depressive symptoms, even if they were bullied.* The data revealed that the intervention specifically affected depressive symptoms of negative mood, feelings of ineffectiveness, and low self-esteem.

Okay, stop. Pause. If you are not completely blown away by this, read it again. This, to me, proves the power of teaching. But also, it proves that Belief is malleable.

To Put It Briefly

The Five Key Beliefs are malleable, which means comments like "So-and-so is just an unmotivated student" aren't the final word. You and I have a big impact on the Five Key Beliefs.

Why It's Important to Know This in a Classroom

It means we can do things about hard circumstances! It means there's hope—lots.

Try This

Think of the rest of this book as a tried and true guide for productively influencing the Five Key Beliefs in the hearts of all of your students.

Credibility

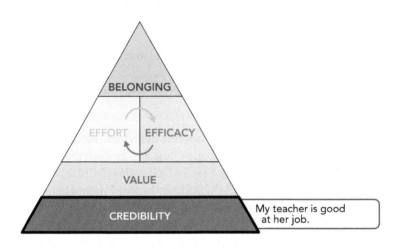

Pyramid levels from top to bottom: BELONGING, EFFORT ⟳ EFFICACY, VALUE, CREDIBILITY

My teacher is good at her job.

WHAT **CREDIBILTY** SOUNDS LIKE IN THE HEART OF A STUDENT	WHAT **ANTI-CREDIBILTY** SOUNDS LIKE IN THE HEART OF A STUDENT
My teacher is good at her job.	I've got a bad teacher.
He knows what he's doing.	He has no idea what he's doing.
She can make a difference for me.	She can't help me.
He cares about me as a person.	He doesn't care about me.
She actually wants me to grow in mastery.	It doesn't matter to her if I grow.
He likes his job.	He hates his job.
There's a fire in her belly for education.	Education for her is just a way to earn a paycheck.
It's fun to watch him work because it's so clear that he likes it.	It's painful watching him work.

Photo by Coryn Wiles

Credibility has the potential to affect all communication events.

—SARA BANFIELD, VIRGINIA RICHMOND, &
JAMES McCROSKEY

When I first came across teacher Credibility in Hattie's (2012) research, I fell in love with its hokey twang. Credibility sounds too good to be true. You're telling me that if students believe that I'm a good teacher, then they'll progress more while they're in my class?

Yes, responds the research. *That is* just *what I'm saying.*

But what's neat is that this goes back waaaaaay further than John Hattie.

- In his *Nichomachaen Ethics*, Aristotle describes credibility as a cornerstone for living one's best life; he describes courage and self-restraint as the foundational virtues beneath credibility and claims that the lived virtues beneath credibility were generosity, magnificence, greatness of soul, balanced ambition, gentleness (concerning anger), friendship, honesty, charm, and the absence of shame (Neill, 2016).

- In their paper "The Eightfold Path of Buddhism for an Effective and Credible Leadership," researchers Shree and Sharma (2014) describe how pursuit of the Eightfold Path is closely aligned with the development of Credibility.

- In his paper "Confucian Trustworthiness and the Practice of Business in China," researcher Koehn (2001) describes the Confucian emphasis on being trustworthy—that is, being credible. According to Koehn, "It is not the failure of others to appreciate your abilities that should trouble you, but rather your own lack of them."

- Upon the conclusion of the famous Sermon on the Mount, the Apostle Matthew records an interesting comment from amongst those listening to the teaching: "When Jesus had finished saying these things, the crowds were amazed at his teaching, because he taught as one who had *authority*, and not as their teachers of the law" (vv. 7:28-29, New International Version). That word *authority* comes from the Greek word ἐξουσίαν, which denotes competence or mastery (Strong, 2010). Basically, folks marveled at his Credibility.

In other words: Credibility's impact in life and learning has been at play a long time. Having established that, let's begin to explore key understandings that will help us cultivate Credibility in our classrooms.

Teachers Are Signal-Senders.

When you're working to be credible, you've got to think of yourself as a kind of radio tower.

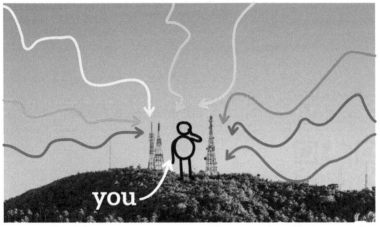

pexels.com/Alexis Ricardo Alaurin

Every word you say, look you give, poster you hang, lesson you teach, and response you offer is a signal to your students. Your aim, from a Credibility standpoint, is to make the bulk of these signals Credibility-conducive.

Credibility-Conducive Signals Come Down to CCP: Care, Competence, and Passion.

The most important mental tool I can give you for Credibility is to focus on CCP: care, competence, and passion. The degree to which you consistently signal these three things to an individual student is the degree to which they are likely to find you a credible teacher.

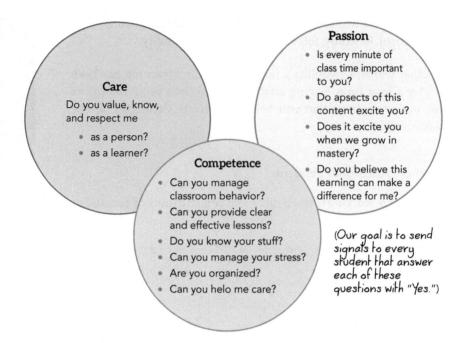

Care

Do you value, know, and respect me

- as a person?
- as a learner?

Competence

- Can you manage classroom behavior?
- Can you provide clear and effective lessons?
- Do you know your stuff?
- Can you manage your stress?
- Are you organized?
- Can you helo me care?

Passion

- Is every minute of class time important to you?
- Do apsects of this content excite you?
- Does it excite you when we grow in mastery?
- Do you believe this learning can make a difference for me?

(Our goal is to send signals to every student that answer each of these questions with "Yes.")

The "CCP" Signals of Credibility: Care, Competence, & Passion

Scan the QR code to view a printable PDF of the CCP diagram.

The diagram above can be helpful in a couple of ways:

- You can print and post it next to your teacher workstation (for a printable PDF, visit https://davestuartjr.com/WTL-Companion).

- You can guide yourself or your team in self-reflection: Where on these lists do I send excellent and consistent signals right now? Where might my signalling be currently weak?

While the research presents other ways for thinking about Credibility's factors—most prominently, Fisher et al.'s (2020) *Teacher Credibility and Collective Efficacy Playbook*—I find CCP to be the best possible simplification. However, if you're not careful to apply the following key understandings, you may not get the Credibility gains you're after. With CCP, take note of the following:

- In order for care signals to contribute to Credibility, the teacher needs to signal that a student is cared for *both* personally (e.g., by showing interest in hobbies, interests, pets, family, extracurriculars) and academically (e.g., by inquiring about grades, learning behaviors, performance tasks, enjoyment of school).

- A teacher need not be perfectly competent in all areas listed above—no teacher I've met is, and I'm certainly not—but in general, these bulleted areas within the circles are most salient to students. When teachers are starting out, I recommend that they select *one* of the bulleted areas per quarter to improve upon. This is so important that we'll dedicate an entire strategy to it (see Strategy 2: Improve at One Thing).

- Passion is more than enthusiasm; it's a tangible fire in the teacher's belly for the students to grow, learn, advance, and deepen. (We'll examine this at length in Strategy 3: Gentle Urgency).

Beware the Tacky Ten

One of my favorite threads of the research on Credibility focuses on the *mis*behaviors of teachers—that is, the things teachers do that hurt student motivation and learning. For example, in Kearney et al. (1991), three categories of teacher misbehavior were identified:

- Incompetence misbehaviors, which "communicate that a teacher does not care about the course or the students" (p. 205). Examples include boring or confusing lectures, unfair tests, or lack of knowledge about the content.

- Indolence misbehaviors, which indicate laziness and disregard for students. Examples include not showing up for class, forgetting assignments or test dates, or failing to grade assignments in a timely manner.

- Offensiveness misbehaviors, such as being unfair, rude, or condescending.

QUESTIONS FOR IDENTIFYING INCOMPETENCE MISBEHAVIORS	QUESTIONS FOR IDENTIFYING INDOLENCE MISBEHAVIORS	QUESTIONS FOR IDENTIFYING OFFENSIVENESS MISBEHAVIORS
The next time you provide direct instruction (the secondary equivalent of a lecture), pay attention. How long did your instruction last? How many students put their heads down or seemed to zone out?	How frequently are you late or absent for class?	If I were to ask your students how fair you are as a teacher, what do you think they would say? Think across the spectrums of their diversity.
Look at your tests. Are they fair? Are they needlessly confusing? Can you answer with a clear conscience, "This question belongs on this test because ___?"	Do you forget assignments? How about test dates? How often do you move test dates?	When you feel rudely treated by a student, do you respond in kind? When you're in a poor mood, are you still polite to students?
Keep track of the questions students ask you about course content. Do you feel confident in your answers? Are your answers clear? Are you able to use understandable analogies to explain?	How long does it typically take you to grade or give feedback on student work? How do your students seem to perceive the average length of time it takes for them to get feedback?	In your heart, do you look down on any of your students? When students ask a question that appears obvious to you, do you take care to honor the question or might condescension come out in the tone of your response?

Though researchers examined many teacher misbehaviors within these subcategories, I like to invite colleagues to focus on improving what I call the Tacky Ten—ten behaviors that are common to all of us but that we can improve through practice and refinement.

The Tacky Ten

CREDIBILITY-HARMING MISBEHAVIOR	MOVING TOWARD SOLUTION
1. Humiliating students	Keep in mind that humiliation is subjective; even if you never intend to embarrass or humiliate a student, you may nonetheless do so. The key, then, is to identify when we accidentally humiliate a student and do what we can to repair the harm done.
2. Intimidating students	Think twice before using "the evil eye" as a classroom stewardship tactic.
3. Acting in a condescending manner	Be careful with go-to pet names for secondary students (e.g., *honey, sweetie*) and be mindful of your tone toward students asking questions.
4. Using sarcasm to get your point across	The older I get, the more I see sarcasm as an unnecessary tool for working well with students or finding humor in life and work. Your mileage may vary, but whatever you do, don't use sarcasm to make a serious point.
5. Forgetting or moving test dates	Create a schedule at the beginning of each semester and plan units according to the schedule. Pretend that the schedule has been set by your boss and it's your job to keep it.
6. Confusing students when you answer their questions or provide direct instruction	Check for understanding multiple times during your lessons.
7. Boring students with your answers to their questions or your direct instruction	I'm the last guy to recommend that you pizzazz up your interactive lectures or direct instruction artificially, but too many teachers needlessly bore students by being long-winded or tangential.
8. Taking a long time to grade assignments	Grade as few assignments as you can—this whole book is an effort to help you move your classrooms away from students being motivated by grades—and for those that you do grade, set time aside on the day you collect the work to get as much of it done as you can.
9. Unfair or confusing tests	Every test you give should be first taken by you, even if you are the one who created the test. This "dogfooding" (Gonzalez, 2015) will help you identify problem areas before your students stumble upon them.
10. Time wasted in lessons	Take pains to develop clear procedures for the beginning, middle, and end of lessons. (See Strategy 2 on page 64 for more on this.)

Beware Your Blind Spots, Especially if You Are Credible With a Good Number of Students.

Once you sense that you are liked by a good number of your students, it can start to feel like you've got the Crediblity thing established. Being liked by students is like a siren song; it's a nice feeling, and it can lure you into complacency. There are two problems with this situation.

First, it's important to remember that Credibility isn't about being *liked*. It's about being judged as good at your job, being judged as someone who can take your students to someplace good—a place of growth in your discipline—that in their hearts they yearn to go. (And yes, beneath even the coolest of too-cool-for-school veneers, I'm convinced there's the heart of a child that longs to learn.)

It certainly *helps* to be liked by your students, *so long as* being liked doesn't hijack your ego. But *it's not necessarily required*. What we're after is something more nuanced than being *liked*—something deeper and stronger and more educationally impactful.

Second, Credibility isn't a "most of them" game. It's about *every one*. We must always remember that teacher Credibility is something we're trying to cultivate in the hearts of *every one* of our students—not just the students we have the easiest time gaining rapport with. We can't be satisfied with signalling care just to the nice kids or the nerdy kids or the athletic kids or the artsy kids—we have to signal this to *all* of them.

Credibility Is the Invisible Ink in All the Teacher Books.

The next time you read a book or a blog written by a teacher-author, here's something to remember: The reason that things work in their class is likely just as much a function of their Credibility with students as it is a function of the quality of the things they do in their class.

What I mean is that when, say, Penny Kittle holds a reading/writing workshop in a high school English language arts (ELA) classroom, one of the reasons why it works literal miracles in her room is because she's a master teacher who is resoundingly, outrageously, cataclysmically good at her job. She has long been a master of the fundamentals of CCP. She signals them without even trying to. She demonstrates her Credibility in every daily lesson, in a week of lessons, and all year long. And on that one accidental instance per school year when she signals anti-Credibility, she knows how to repair the damage.

And the word of her teacher power gets out to the students. What results is a good kind of snowballing, where more and more people in the community believe she's a good teacher, and this in turn makes it easier for her to keep improving (after all, it's motivating to have people believe in you). This is why teacher Credibility is the number one way to start improving student motivation in your room, bar none. It's the foundation at the bottom of the Five Key Beliefs pyramid for a reason. Wise are those who study it!

Now, none of this is to say that the reading/writing workshop model Kittle uses for her ELA classes *only* works because of her high Credibility. Reading/writing workshop is brilliant and deep and empowering and connective, and if Penny Kittle began teaching courses at my high school, I'd be the first to sign up. I'd want all my children to sign up, too. I'm just saying that the approaches you read about in teacher-author books are not the only factors influencing the motivation and growth of that teacher's students. Credibility exerts a massive influence as well.

In other words, take pains to think as clearly as you can about teacher Credibility—what it is, how judgments of it are formed in the hearts of students—even as you're taking pains to learn about reading/ writing workshops, or modeling-based science, or "ditch the textbook" initiatives (a "baby with the bathwater" notion, in my opinion), or presidential fitness tests in physical education. If you want to get the most out of new or old books or initiatives, study up on Credibility!

Credibility Isn't About Being Popular or Cool.

I clearly remember, early in my career, how good it made me feel to hear a student say, "Mr. Stuart, you're my favorite teacher." It was like an amphetamine for the ego. I was hooked on that rush and driven by it.

This ego-fuelled addiction, however, had some unfortunate side effects:

- Some of my savvier students likely sensed how easy it was to manipulate me with this kind of praise.

- Students who really meant statements like this were becoming dependent on me and my particular teaching style in ways that wouldn't help them long-term in their education.

- Since there can only be one favorite, praise like this was making me competitive with my colleagues in ways that served no good end.

- The tenuousness of being the favorite meant that I was constantly pushing myself beyond the level of helpful stress and I was constantly looking for more time to work.

Ultimately, I ended up quitting teaching for one year following my third year on the job. There was a lot that went into that decision, but part of it was likely the drain on my soul that came from being so enamored of this fleeting kind of comparative praise.

Credibility, thankfully, has nothing at all to do with favorite or best or comparison. This is one of my favorite things about the belief: All teachers in a school can be Credible, whereas only one can be a particular student's favorite.

So, if you too find yourself chasing after being the favorite, start to tell yourself this truth: Crediblity has nothing at all to do with that, and you'd be better off viewing such praise with the same bemused fondness as you might a student's proffered doodle that they made during class.

And, if you have found yourself jealous of teachers more popular or "cool" than you, take heart: That's all dust in the wind compared to the powerful, attainable Credibility belief that we're exploring in these pages.

Not All Kinds of Competence Equally Impact Your Credibility.

I like to use the following diagram to help teachers understand which areas of their practice are most likely to influence students' perceptions of their Credibility. On the left side of the diagram you have areas of practice that your students will sense on a daily basis: classroom stewardship; student motivation and engagement; basic, effective lesson preparation; and how students learn. On the right side, you have areas of practice that are less immediately sensed by students but that nonetheless heavily influence their long-term perception of you: professional knowledge, teacher stress management, working well with adults, and teacher time management. In Strategy 2, I'll advise you to master these eight things before getting involved with other, more specialized areas.

Domains of Teacher Competence That Most Influence Credibility Signalling

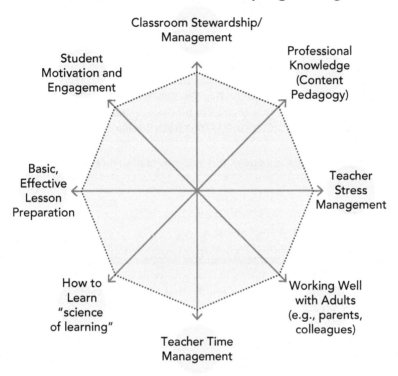

Classroom Stewardship/ Management

Professional Knowledge (Content Pedagogy)

Student Motivation and Engagement

Basic, Effective Lesson Preparation

Teacher Stress Management

How to Learn "science of learning"

Working Well with Adults (e.g., parents, colleagues)

Teacher Time Management

COMMON TEACHER HANG-UPS

My Students Come to Me From a Colleague Whom They Describe as Clearly Noncredible. Does This Hurt My Credibility?

Unfortunately, yes. Our same-building colleagues shape the larger context of our school, and therefore when they are perceived by students as bad at their jobs, we are likely to see a reduction in our own Credibility with at least some students.

(Continued)

(Continued)

The quickest way that a colleague can begin to remedy this is via tracking moment of genuine connection (MGC) attempts (see Strategy 1) and focusing on improving their practice in the weakness area that is most negatively impacting their Credibility (see Strategy 2). Unfortunately, I have not discovered the secret to making a colleague care about improving in these areas, though I suspect it has something to do with the Five Key Beliefs. I have seen many administrators take the Five Key Beliefs approach outlined in this book, modify it for noncredible teachers on their faculty, and slowly but surely cultivate improvements in teacher motivation.

So, get your boss a copy of this book and tell them to get to work. :)

I'm Brand New to Teaching and Feel Like I'm Incompetent Everywhere.

The good news is, you're wrong! You're totally competent in some places. For example, take a look at your body right now. Is it clothed? Nice! I'm guessing you did that. Were your teeth brushed today? Great!

I know that's a bit cheeky, but it's important for your own motivation to keep your perspective on not just your inadequacies but also the things you are good at. To take a more serious angle, consider the last week of your practice:

- Is there a student whose day you made just a bit brighter?

- Is there a new concept you learned in your discipline or a new way of explaining that concept to students?

- Is there a neat tidbit you picked up from personal research about schooling or life or your discipline?

The first step to solving this hang-up is realizing that you're not sitting stationary. The next and much harder step, of course, is to start improving, specifically on the aspects of teaching that are most impactful on how you experience the daily classroom. We'll dive deeply into all of that in Strategy 2.

I Don't Like What I'm Teaching!

In my conversations with colleagues and my reflection on my own career so far, I see two general areas where a dislike of what we're teaching can come from:

1. personal taste—for example, when I was teaching English 9 a few years back, it took me a while to get over my dislike of Bradbury's style in *Fahrenheit 451*—and

2. professional disagreement—for example, a science teacher using a traditional curriculum who believes all learning should be phenomenon-focused; a math teacher given a textbook to teach from who believes in the "experience first, formalize later" method of math instruction; or an English teacher given a curriculum with whole-class text units (e.g., Shakespeare's *Romeo and Juliet* for a ninth-grade course) who believes that all reading should be student-selected.

Obviously, these two issues have different solutions. For both problem areas, I encourage teachers to begin by trying the "Gimme Ten Reasons It's Good" exercise. In matters of personal taste, this is often the exercise that you need to keep on doing and doing.

 Scan this QR code for a walkthrough of "Gimme Ten Reasons It's Good".

But in matters of professional disagreement, if you keep teaching something that you believe is wrong-headed or deleterious to student growth, you'll eventually find yourself deeply demoralized. Just as it's harmful to our students' souls when they are required to do things each day that they do not believe in, so too it is harmful to ours.

However, as we see all throughout the book you're holding, beliefs are malleable things; they can be changed given the right knowledge and experiences and signals. Before you go seeking another job or career, then, I recommend that you do that hard

(Continued)

(Continued)

work of determining if your professional conclusions are truly the "correct" ones—or are they just the closely held opinions of a vociferous segment of teachers on social media or at the hot conference in your content area?

My background is mostly in ELA instruction, and I remember early on in my researching days being fairly convinced that the only kind of good reading was reading chosen by a student. I thought that whole-class texts were an affront to human dignity and just downright malpractical. But then I got curious. I found books like Ariel Sacks's (2014) *Whole Novels for the Whole Class*. I gained understanding of the role that knowledge plays in culture development from works such as Daniel Coyle's (2018) *Culture Code*. I learned about broad-level reading comprehension from writings such as Daniel Willingham's (2006) article "How Knowledge Helps." Over time, I realized that despite hot-take tweets of prominent voices in the choice-reading world, choice reading had some significant drawbacks when taken to the extremes I once believed in.

So, do some extra research, particularly outside of intradisciplinary echo chambers, before you set your professional views in stone. It'll make the job a lot more fun and interesting.

I Think I Sent a Lot of Anti-Credibility Signals to My Students Early in the School Year. I'm Done for, Right?

There's lots of hype around the first days of school, as well there ought to be. You don't get a second chance at a first impression, right?

But the good news with Credibility is that it's a long-term game. No matter how your first week goes, or your next week, or the week after that, what matters most is asking yourself, *How am I going to signal to my students that I am Credible today?* How can I signal care and competence and passion to the individuals I teach right now?

In other words, while it's true that first days have special characteristics in the hearts of our students, it's mostly in the humdrum where Credibility is made or lost.

Strategy 1: Track Attempted MGCs

A moment of genuine connection (MGC) is any situation where you briefly interact with a student and you attempt to communicate, earnestly and simply, that you value, know, or respect that student. Because feelings of being valued, known, and respected are subjective, a teacher can't expect to control whether a student feels these ways after a brief interaction. Hence, to enact this strategy we don't seek to *guarantee* an MGC but instead to guarantee that we are regularly *attempting* MGCs with each student we teach.

What to Do

- Before class, during an independent work portion of class, or after class, pull aside students and attempt to make them feel valued, known, and respected (examples below).

- As you do this, keep track of who you've done it with (example tracking systems below).

- Don't repeat an MGC attempt with a student until you've attempted an MGC with every student on your roster; this discipline is important for establishing an equitable, "student-by-student ground game" that signals care to every individual.

- When you sense in your heart that there's a student you're coming to not value or respect (this happens to most of us, myself included), work to again value and respect that student; this is the *genuine* part of MGC. MGCs don't work when they're faked.

Key Pointer

- In order for your MGC attempts to contribute to your teacher credibility, it's important to balance your attempts between academic and personal connections. For example, personal attempts might include the following:

  - Adam, I remember that you like the Michigan Wolverines. Did you watch the game this past Saturday? Yikes—that was a tough loss for us.

- ○ Bianca, how did your dance recital go this past weekend? I saw that you wrote about it in your warm-up last week. I'm impressed that you balance both school and such a rigorous extracurricular activity!
- And academic attempts might look something like these:
  - ○ Charlie, how has your at-home instrument practice been going? Where are you having a hard time or getting stuck? I'm glad you're in my music class, and I want to do whatever I can to help you in your efforts to improve.
  - ○ Danielle, what goals do you have for yourself in school during this new semester? How can I be a support as you pursue these?

How Strategy 1 Influences the Five Key Beliefs

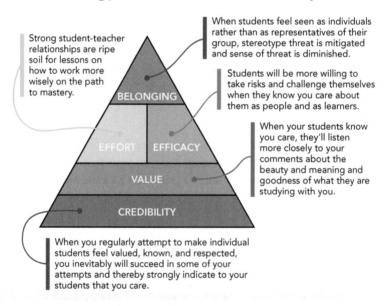

Strong student-teacher relationships are ripe soil for lessons on how to work more wisely on the path to mastery.

When students feel seen as individuals rather than as representatives of their group, stereotype threat is mitigated and sense of threat is diminished.

Students will be more willing to take risks and challenge themselves when they know you care about them as people and as learners.

When your students know you care, they'll listen more closely to your comments about the beauty and meaning and goodness of what they are studying with you.

BELONGING

EFFORT EFFICACY

VALUE

CREDIBILITY

When you regularly attempt to make individual students feel valued, known, and respected, you inevitably will succeed in some of your attempts and thereby strongly indicate to your students that you care.

WHY THIS STRATEGY

I've got about a million reasons why tracking MGC attempts is worth your time. I mean, that's what this book is all about: the teaching techniques that are most worth your time. Each of our ten focus strategies, if you practice toward expertise in them, will make your classroom richer with the Five Key Beliefs in uniquely powerful ways. But to keep the book streamlined, I'll limit my remarks right now to just the top five reasons why I think you've got to go big on tracking attempted MGCs.

This Strategy Helps You to *See* Your Students as the Once-in-a-Universe Souls That They Are.

Like so much of teaching, the person who gains the most out of Strategy 1 is the teacher. That's because as I practice the discipline of communicating that I value, know, and respect all of my students as individuals, my heart and mind become trained *away* from abstracting them into generic numbers on my roster and *toward* marvelling at their stupendous originality.

This Strategy Helps You Remember Why You're a Teacher to Begin With.

There's this line in the old Hebrew poem, "Psalm 139," where the writer proclaims, "I praise you because I am fearfully and wonderfully made; your works are wonderful, I know that full well." I've always loved that language, "fearfully and wonderfully made." It speaks to universal human dignity. The word *fearful* can be confusing though; it's not an anxious fear, but instead the kind of thing you feel standing at the edge of the Grand Canyon or listening to the roar of Niagara Falls.

I only bring this up because this strategy helps us grow in our tendency to see students as fearfully and wonderfully wrought. In turn, we'll find it easier to remember that what we're doing matters and is worth the difficulty that often attends it. Is the system broken? Often so. Are the conditions rough? They certainly can be. Can our students challenge us? You bet. But gosh—the work is good.

This Strategy Draws the Ellies out of the Alienation Whirlpool.

Years ago, I taught a student whom I'll call Ellie. I wish you could have seen Ellie's standard facial expressions in my classroom the first six months I taught her. She exuded an aura that said to me, "This teacher is a joke. I can't stand this guy. He's out of touch. He's old.

He's lame." Each time I pulled Ellie aside for an MGC attempt, she just didn't seem to want to talk to me.

There was one day in particular when I asked Ellie to step into the hallway during an independent-work portion of class.[10] In this case, my MGC plan was to talk to her about her grades.

"Hey Ellie, how are you today?"

"Fine."

"Good! Ellie, I'm just checking in with students this week on how school is going in general. How are your grades in all your classes?"

"Fine."

"What kinds of letters did you see in PowerSchool the last time you checked?"

"*C*s and *D*s. One *E*."

"Oh—how do you feel about that?"

"Fine."

"Well, listen, I'm going to be honest with you Ellie, because I think that's important. Those grades don't sound to me like they line up with who you are and where I sense that you're going. I'm not a 'grades are all that matters' type, not at all. But you and I both know you're capable of more than that. Right?"

"I guess."

"Well listen, if you ever want to have a quiet place to work on things for any of your classes, you just let me know, all right? My room is quiet during lunches and after school most days; I'd happily open the

---

[10]This pulling a student out into the hallway is a positive norm in my class-room. By the end of the first month of school, all students have been pulled out at least once for a brief conversation, and most of these conversations are intentionally aimed at being encouraging.

door for you and any other classmates that you think may want to come and get work done. Square deal?"

"Okay."

Ellie went back inside. I marked on my clipboard an A next to Ellie's name, meaning I had attempted an academic MGC with her. And the day moved on.

Later that afternoon, I got a call from my principal.

"Mr. Stuart, Ellie was in a fight this afternoon, and your name came up just now when I was talking with her. Ellie shared with me a lot of things that have been going on with her outside of school, and it was a lot of really hard stuff. And I asked her, 'Hey, is there anyone at school that you can talk to when this stuff becomes too overwhelming?' And she replied, 'Yes. I can talk to Mr. Stuart.'"

Wait, I thought. *Me? The guy she can't seem to stand?*

My reason for sharing this story isn't that I think I'm some kind of special teacher. I'm sharing it for these reasons:

- If I hadn't been tracking MGC attempts, the awkwardness of my attempts with Ellie would have undoubtedly led me to seek fewer connections with her than I should have. She would have been one of those students that is in the classroom, is not causing major problems, and is left to herself.

- Because I had been tracking MGC attempts, by this point in the school year Ellie had experienced ten or so brief moments with me in which I just tried to communicate to her heart: "Ellie, I see you, I value you, I know you, I respect you. I'm glad you're in my class." And while many of those attempts likely failed, at least a couple apparently did not.

That is how tracked MGC attempts work. That is how, over time, they lead to noticeable gains in Credibility because the Ellies of your school aren't being missed. This gives you a reputation for caring in a special way for all of your students, and you become well-loved in all student subgroups.

The Alienation Whirlpool

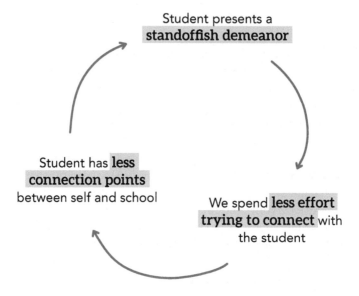

Student presents a
standoffish demeanor

Student has **less
connection points**
between self and school

We spend **less effort
trying to connect** with
the student

When we don't track MGC attempts for our full rosters, we can end up approaching students who appear standoffish or annoyed less than we should—kind of like the story I shared about Ellie above.

This Strategy Is the Most Efficient Method Ever for Building Strong Working Relationships With All of Your Students.

I remember when I was in my twenties meeting with a financial advisor in the cafeteria of my first school placement. It was one of those "free pizza lunch as long as you listen to the personal finance guy's spiel" things. Obviously having been hooked by free pizza, I was there when the advisor shared a compound interest graph we've all seen before.

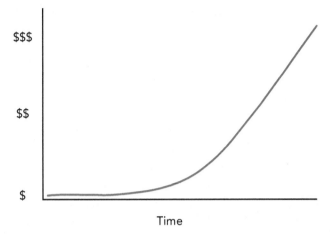

"The best way to unlock this power," said the finance guy, "is to invest without even thinking about it—that is, to have money automatically withdrawn from all of your paychecks and placed into your investment account. If you start this young, it'll seem like nothing at first, but eventually . . . I mean, just look at the chart."

In my experience, this is a lot like how Strategy 1 works. You make tiny and regular investments in your relationships with each of your students—one thirty-to-sixty-second attempted MGC at a time—and within a few months you realize, *Wow, I've got functioning teacher-student relationships with all of my students, and I've not spent that much time creating them.* MGCs, it turns out, are the basic building block of a relationships-rich classroom environment.

In the first three years of my career, I believed that in order to have strong working relationships with my students I needed to have my classroom door open all of the time. So before school, during lunch, and after school for hours there would be at least a handful of students in my classroom. When I look back and do the math, it's safe to say that I spent fifteen to twenty hours per week building relationships with students.

And, truly—we had great relationships!

The trouble was, of course, that those fifteen to twenty hours didn't come from nowhere. They were hours in which I wasn't analyzing student work, wasn't providing feedback, wasn't planning lessons, wasn't doing research into the craft, and wasn't collaborating with my colleagues on how to improve toward competence. Because of this, there was never an evening when I didn't bring work home with me, never a weekend untouched by the labors of the classroom.

Eventually, I had all the marks of classic burnout: I felt overstretched, incompetent, and ineffective. So I quit teaching. While my wife was finishing her undergraduate degree in New York City, I worked odd jobs that had nothing to do with school. I bussed tables, barista'ed coffee drinks, answered phones, and sold comedy club tickets. It was exhausting and unfulfilling, and by the end of that year, I sensed that I was meant for a classroom. However, I also realized that, should I return to teaching, I was going to need to find a way to do it sustainably. I was going to need to be able to both be a good teacher *and* have a full life in the evenings and on the weekends.

Tracking MGC attempts was one of the key initial building blocks of this new approach to teaching. What used to take me fifteen to twenty hours per week now took me fifteen to thirty seconds (per student) every two weeks.

I haven't turned back since. And, strangely, I would describe my relationships with students *now* as immensely more productive than my relationships with students back when I was the open-door guy. When my door is closed and I'm working on my craft or my lessons or feedback on student work, I'm becoming really good at my job. And when students are with me during their class periods, I'm strategically building meaningful and strong working relationships one brief MGC attempt at a time.

This Strategy Is So Obvious That 95 Percent of Us Overlook It.

Now, before we move into practicalities, let's address something you may be sensing: MGC attempts are an obvious strategy. So obvious, in fact, that some may find it insulting. As in, "Did I seriously take the time to pick up a book that is going to tell me I need to attempt to make students feel valued, known, and respected? That's Teaching 101, man!"

And herein we have one of my greatest communicative challenges so far in this book: I'm explaining to you something that you already know how to do and already know is important, but at the same time it's a strategy that is grossly underutilized by the average classroom teacher.

Some muscular-albeit-anecdotal evidence: In 2021–2022, I asked every teacher audience I spoke to, "Would you mind raising your hand if you've kept track of the students with whom you've attempted an MGC in the past month of your practice?" Less than 1 percent of respondents said they had, out of a total audience pool of several thousand colleagues.

Here's the key leverage point of the strategy: All of us know we're supposed to try making students feel valued, known, and respected. But about 99 percent of us have no way of knowing whether we've *actually done this* for the students on our roster in a given year.

In an elementary classroom, it may make sense not to keep track of attempted MGCs. Such teachers may have redundant mechanisms— meaning mechanism upon mechanism, so that no odd event can preclude their proper functioning. I don't know as I've never taught elementary students in a public school classroom setting.

But, in a secondary teacher's student load, where there are one to two hundred students on a total day's roster? It's *insanity* to not have a tracking mechanism for this critical Credibility signal. According to American-Canadian psychologist Levitin (2015), "Writing things down conserves the mental energy expended in worrying that you might forget something and in trying not to forget it" (p. 67).

Tracking MGCs, then, is a no-brainer; after all, who among us needs to waste a single ounce of mental energy?

HOW TO GAIN PROFICIENCY WITH STRATEGY 1

As with all of the ten strategies in this book, tracking MGC attempts isn't like pushing a button on a machine. It's a learnable, improvable, refinable *skill*. Our first goal is for you to become so proficient at it that it becomes like driving a car or tying your shoes. Automaticity in this, like in all things, will be the fruit of practice.

Step One: Print the Doggone Paper.

I like to keep track of my MGC attempts using a simple, single-sheet roster. I copy and paste student names from PowerSchool into this Google Sheet (see next page) and then print ten or so copies. In my Google Drive, I label this sheet, creatively, Clipboard Sheet. As my roster changes during the year—as students join or leave the school—I update this single document and print out fresh copies.

Scan the QR code to view/download the Google Sheet that I use as a Clipboard Sheet

HOUR 1			HOUR 2			HOUR 3		
Student			Student			Student		
Student			Student			Student		
Student			Student			Student		
Student			Student			Student		
Student			Student			Student		
Student			Student			Student		
Student			Student			Student		
Student			Student			Student		
Student			Student			Student		
Student			Student			Student		
Student			Student			Student		
Student			Student			Student		
Student			Student			Student		
Student			Student			Student		
Student			Student			Student		
Student			Student			Student		
Student			Student			Student		
Student			Student			Student		
Student			Student			Student		
Student			Student			Student		
Student			Student			Student		
Student			Student			Student		
Student			Student			Student		
Student			Student			Student		
Student			Student			Student		
Student			Student			Student		
Student			Student			Student		
Student			Student			Student		
Student			Student			Student		
Student			Student			Student		
Student			Student			Student		
Student			Student			Student		

Others like to keep track on a seating chart. For example, here's Clint Roberts's MGC tracker from his practice as a band instructor at Oak Canyon Junior High School in Linden, Utah.

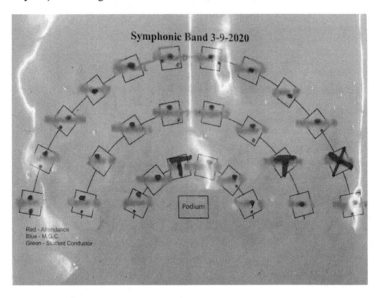

Here's how Clint describes it:

> I wanted to run with your concept of "Moments of Genuine Connection" tracking sheet but in context for band. At the beginning of the year I was cutting out student photos and scanning them to create a seating chart. It took forever but was worth it to put students' faces and names together. Now that I have those names and faces, I use https://bgreco.net/band to generate my band seating charts.
>
> After printing the chart, I put it into a clear sheet in my attendance binder that stays on my conductor's music stand. I take roll with a red dry erase marker and erase it each day when it goes in the computer. I'll be using Blue and Green to mark which students have had certain opportunities in class. Blue dots will be students with whom I've had an MGC. Green dots will be students who have had an opportunity to conduct the band either in warm-ups or a song (my class's version of public speaking).

Some folks do this digitally, too—for example, here's a spreadsheet Dr. Charles Youngs, an English department chair in Pennsylvania, developed during the early pandemic.

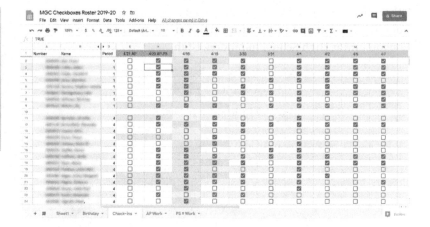

Scan the QR code to get a copy of Dr. Youngs's MGC Checkboxes spreadsheet.

Step Two: Set a Tempo.

You want to make sure that you attempt MGCs regularly, and to help with that you need to set a tempo. As a practical example, for secondary teachers with five to six class periods per day and thirty to forty students per class period, I recommend aiming for three MGC attempts per class period per day. In my practice, this often looks like this:

- one attempt while students are filtering into class,
- one during an independent work portion of the class (often the written lesson warm-up for me), and
- one as students are filtering out of class.[11]

If you do this on a daily basis, you'll have an MGC attempt with thirty students per two-week period for each of the classes you teach. This means that, in a given school year of forty weeks, you'll

---

[11]Keep in mind that in each of these interactions I'm pulling the target student aside or out into the hallway. I want these to be as private as they can be.

end up attempting an MGC with every one of your students fifteen to twenty times, depending on how big your classes are. That is a *lot* of attempts! Inevitably, a few of them are going to land square in the hearts of your target students. Credibility, here we come!

Step Three: Track Every MGC Attempt.

After I attempt an MGC with a student, I make a simple notation on my clipboard sheet. If I attempted to make the student feel valued, known, or respected academically, I mark an *A*; otherwise, I mark a *P* for personal. This is something I spend zero seconds overthinking; I just mark it down and move on.

Over time, the *A*s and *P*s give me a sense of how well I'm balancing my attempts between personal and academic. This is important, as too many *personal* attempts will make you a nice person in the eyes of the student but not necessarily a good teacher. If you're trying to improve student motivation, you need to be perceived of as someone *more* than nice or caring; you need to be perceived of as a *good teacher*. And so you must balance the *A*s and the *P*s.

A Few More Pointers for Gaining Proficiency With Strategy 1

Practice in the mirror. I often hear from folks about how their MGCs can be awkward (see the common teacher hang-ups on page 61), and while bit of that is inevitable, some of it does have to do with our own skill and confidence. The quickest way to fix this, apart from just getting your reps in with the students in your class, is to practice five or so MGCs per day in the mirror as you're getting ready for work. It may feel silly, but just imagine that you're an athlete or performer preparing for something important and hard.

Rehearsal is key!

Incorporate MGC attempts into your teacher evaluation goals. If there's any way for you to work MGC attempts into your teacher evaluations, you should. This lets you turn what is often a hoop jump—being evaluated on an overly complex teaching rubric on whether or not you're a proficient teacher—into something that aligns with actual competency development.

When you find that you don't like a student, work on that. I often mention on my blog and in my workshops that I don't naturally like all of my students. For some of them, it takes *work*. I don't think this is because I am a jerk; I think it is because I am a human being and so are my students.

What I try to do to remedy this is, first, be mindful of small twinges in my heart as I'm looking at my roster. Is there a student whose name provokes a twinge of anger? Annoyance? Embarrassment? Frustration? Hurt? I make note of that—usually on a blank index card, stacks of which I keep all over my room—and then, later on, I sit down or take a walk to process where that feeling is coming from. Usually I find there's some memory associated with this student that I've been holding on to. These can be as extreme as a student cussing me out—yes, it still does happen to me, even halfway into my career—or as minor as a student laughing at a comment that I made in seriousness.

Once in awhile, try connecting with every student in a day. When I sense a lull in my soul about the work of teaching, sometimes I rearrange my lesson plans so that I can attempt an MGC with every student that I teach in a single class period. Since my classes have thirty to forty students in them every hour, this of course takes some finagling.

Typically it means I'll need to use an extended independent work block in the lesson. In order for this to be an effective use of learning time for all students, the work at hand needs to be something that my students can navigate on their own. In my world history classes, this may be an extended set of primary source documents with accompanying analysis scaffolding questions (the DBQ Project publishes fine examples of these). In my ELA classes, this may be an extended segment of independent reading or writing.

As students are doing this, I ask one of them at a time to step into the hallway for a thirty-to-sixty-second chat. This gives me lots of MGC attempt reps in a short amount of time, which is great for my skill-building in this area. It also gives me a motivation boost as I'm reminded of just how special my students are.

Our colleague Linda Bisarek, an instructional coach in Hillsboro, Wisconsin, honors teacher requests to cover their classrooms while the teacher pulls students for this kind of periodic everyone-in-a-period MGC spree. If you've got an instructional coach or support personnel at your school that can monitor independent work in your room while you do this, it's a pretty fine opportunity for the coach to have an impact on your practice and your students to gain something special from a day of class.[12]

COMMON TEACHER HANG-UPS

My MGCs Are Awkward!

I've had colleagues write in to the blog before saying, "Dave, I'm a bit embarrassed to admit this, but sometimes it feels like my MGCs are . . . awkward, like pulling teeth. How do you mitigate this in your classroom?"

I find a few things help here:

- First, take heart in knowing that every secondary educator on the planet has awkward encounters with their students. Adolescents, in their infinite diversity, are a gloriously awkward people group—and I say that with the love and admiration only possible from someone who is himself sometimes more than a bit awkward. While I'm not one to say that we ought to *try making* these encounters awkward—far be that from us—I am certainly of the belief that some of them just will be.

- Second, it is helpful at first to practice MGC attempts in the mirror at home. I know I mentioned this a few sections prior, but it bears repeating. In my conversations with teachers near and far, I find verbal, out-loud practice to be a critically underutilized form of teacher expertise development. If you want to get smoother at delivering these brief thirty-to-sixty-second "I see you" moments to your students, practice them at home in front of a mirror before you head to work.

- And finally, keep at it. The more MGC attempts you check off of your list and the more lists you fill completely, the more adept you'll become at navigating the waters of awkwardness.

(Continued)

---

[12]For a strategy that's sort of like Strategy 1 but focused specifically on students you're most concerned about reaching, see "Common Teacher Hang-Ups: I Have a Student Who Seems Completely Uninterested in Succeeding. What Should I Do?" on page 200.

(Continued)

I Did an MGC With a Student, but It Didn't Work!

Too often, books and trainings for teachers treat our job as if we're technicians: "Use *X* strategy and you'll get *Y* result, every time—results guaranteed!" Given the complexity of a student's soul, this is at best a silly notion and at worst deeply demoralizing. Yet silver-bullet promises persist nonetheless.

There are a few things that help us think better about MGC attempts that seem to fail.

- First, like every worthwhile teaching strategy, MGC attempts are a practicable, improvable skill. There are weak MGC attempts and strong MGC attempts. There are ways, absolutely, to do them wrong, such as making them public instead of private. I'm talking about *practice*. Keep at it.

- More importantly, you have to view tracking attempted MGCs as a strategy akin to long-term investing. With each series you complete, the likelihood of a student receiving the valued/respected/known signal into their heart increases.

- Finally, you may need to seek to repair damage done. More on that in the next hang-up.

In short, it's critical to see Strategy 1 not as a one-and-done intervention but instead as a comprehensive, context-shaping approach to teacher-student relationship development.

I've Got a Really Bad Relationship With a Student, and a One-on-One MGC Seems Really Unsafe.

First of all, let me be clear that I don't know your unique situation. Any time that you feel unsafe in your practice, I implore you to reach out to proper supports and protect yourself from danger.

With that said, sometimes I find that MGCs are threatening to me when I know that my relationship with a given student is quite sour. In situations like this, the surest source of relief is an attempted repair of the relationship.

Let's take an example from my practice; we'll call this student Nysha. I noticed one day in class that Nysha's affect toward me was markedly colder than I had noticed before. Not wanting to make assumptions, I noted the difference and resolved to attempt a repair-focused MGC with Nysha at my earliest convenience.

When the chance arrived for me to ask Nysha for a brief conversation in the hallway, I said something like, "Nysha, I've noticed a change in your demeanor toward me lately. I have to ask, have I offended or hurt you in some way? If I have, I'd like to apologize and make it right. My goal is never to offend or humiliate a student, but I'm not silly enough to think that I don't accidentally do just that. Please know that what you share with me, I'll not hold against you, Nysha. I just want you to be comfortable to learn and grow in my classroom."

In this particular case, Nysha did not share anything with me during this attempted MGC, but I found out a day later that she had gone to the school counselor shortly prior and said she did not feel comfortable in my classroom. The reason, it turned out, was that I had asked her a question about her recent gaps in attendance, and from her perspective the way that I asked it was audible to nearby peers and therefore humiliating.[13]

I told the counselor that I was grateful to learn this, and at my earliest opportunity I asked Nysha into the hallway to tell her what the counselor had shared and how sorry I was for making her feel ashamed or embarrassed. Nysha told me that she appreciated my apology and my sensitivity to pull her out the previous day.

I almost always find in situations like this that simply making the moves to reach out and be curious are the majority of what it takes to repair rifts in a relationship.

Given that secondary teachers have upwards of a hundred students that we interact with in a given day, I find it inevitable that we'll offend or embarrass someone at some point in the year. While we shouldn't be complacent and should always seek to improve our sensitivity in this area, we also must remember that part of the job is being mindful of situations where repair is needed.

---

[13]Humiliating students is one of the Tacky Ten we looked at on page 39.

Strategy 2: Improve at One Thing

Teaching has a tendency to draw into its ranks those with grandiose visions of achievement. Some want to be the teacher that they never had; others wish to mimic savior-archetype examples from stories like *Dead Poets Society* or *Freedom Writers*. Some others were rockstars in their school days and now bring an academic workaholism to their careers.

In Strategy 2 we buck our all-or-nothing, perfectionist tendencies and replace them with a dogged determination to *focus*. I find that there are eight key areas of competency that, when acquired, make teaching noticeably better for you and for all of your students. Before allowing ourselves to apprentice to more extraneous competency areas, we must first gain a basic mastery of the eight areas of practice that matter most for creating a classroom environment that is both enjoyable and productive.

What to Do

Give yourself two-or-three-month chunks of time in which you focus your professional development efforts on areas of practice most closely linked with your Credibility. In my estimation, the following eight areas of practice meet those criteria:

1. Classroom stewardship/management
2. Student motivation and engagement
3. Basic, effective lesson preparation
4. How students learn/the "science of learning"
5. Professional knowledge (content, pedagogy)
6. Teacher stress management
7. Working well with adults
8. Teacher time management

We'll unpack all of these further on pages 79–80.

How Strategy 2 Influences the Five Key Beliefs

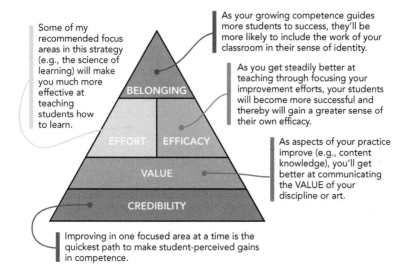

Some of my recommended focus areas in this strategy (e.g., the science of learning) will make you much more effective at teaching students how to learn.

As your growing competence guides more students to success, they'll be more likely to include the work of your classroom in their sense of identity.

As you get steadily better at teaching through focusing your improvement efforts, your students will become more successful and thereby will gain a greater sense of their own efficacy.

As aspects of your practice improve (e.g., content knowledge), you'll get better at communicating the VALUE of your discipline or art.

Improving in one focused area at a time is the quickest path to make student-perceived gains in competence.

WHY THIS STRATEGY

In earlier drafts, I had this section filled with dense analytical reasoning. But then I said, you know what? Let's do this in pictures.

This is us, today, at our current skill level.

This is the time and
energy we have to
expend toward
improving our current
skill level, when
expending equally in
all directions.

This is the line at which our students start seeing noticeable growth in our skill level; it's also the line at which we begin enjoying the good feeling that comes with getting noticeably better at something.

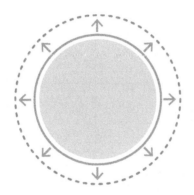

If you do it this way—expending your energy
equally in all possible directions for
improvement—it takes a long time to get to the
enjoyable and Credibility-enhancing purple line.

All right now, let's superimpose our circle of present skill right on top of those 8 domains of competence from several pages ago.

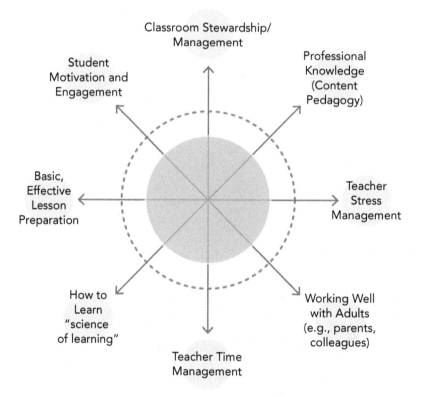

Classroom Stewardship/
Management

Professional
Knowledge
(Content
Pedagogy)

Student
Motivation and
Engagement

Basic,
Effective
Lesson
Preparation

Teacher
Stress
Management

How to
Learn
"science
of learning"

Working Well
with Adults
(e.g., parents,
colleagues)

Teacher Time
Management

This is going to help us understand why Strategy 2: Improve at One Thing is so important.

Now, Here's our time and energy again, but this time I've squished it all so that all its surface area is focused in a single direction.

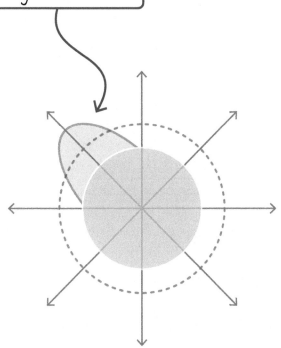

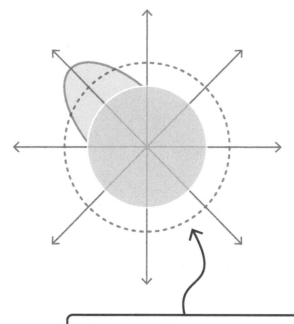

Notice that when we focus that red energy circle, we get to the purple line more quickly. That's great news! After all, this is the line at which our students begin to sense a tangible difference in our competence.

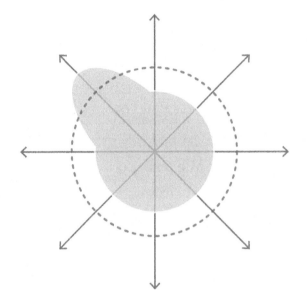

If you do it this way—focusing efforts on one thing at a time—you grow your grey circle a lot more quickly, but the growth is uneven, so . . .

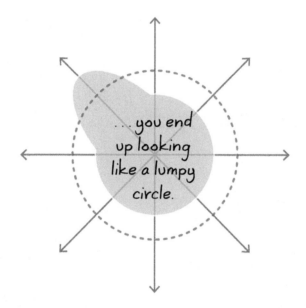

. . . you end up looking like a lumpy circle.

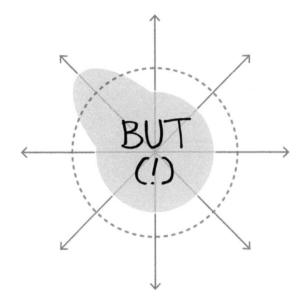

Your lumpiness, by getting you to the purple line more quickly, means that you'll be sending stronger Credibility signals to your students faster . . .

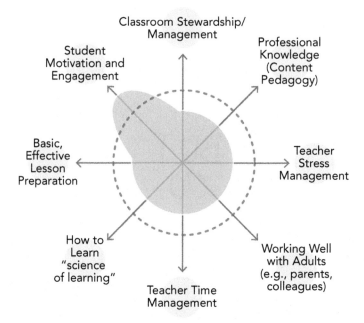

. . . and you'll be enjoying the feeling of getting competent more quickly.

Then you select another single area to improve upon, and on and on you go.

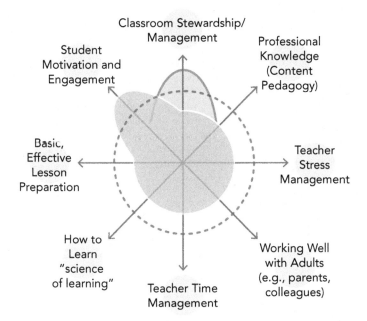

Classroom Stewardship/ Management

Student Motivation and Engagement

Professional Knowledge (Content Pedagogy)

Basic, Effective Lesson Preparation

Teacher Stress Management

How to Learn "science of learning"

Teacher Time Management

Working Well with Adults (e.g., parents, colleagues)

Eventually, all of the competency domains that most influence your Credibilty will be noticeably established in the eyes of your students.

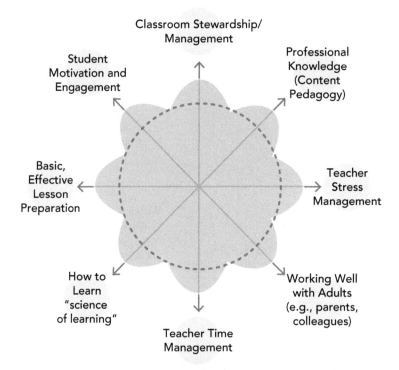

Classroom Stewardship/ Management

Student Motivation and Engagement

Professional Knowledge (Content Pedagogy)

Basic, Effective Lesson Preparation

Teacher Stress Management

How to Learn "science of learning"

Working Well with Adults (e.g., parents, colleagues)

Teacher Time Management

(And you'll like your job more too.)

In short, Strategy 2 is about getting you and your students to the quickest and most critical competency gains possible. It's getting you to the place where you're competent enough in core areas that your students *notice* that competence. It makes your students' time in your room more enjoyable, as all students prefer being in the presence of a competent teacher, and it makes *your* time in your room more enjoyable, as we all prefer doing things that we're competent at.

HOW TO GAIN PROFICIENCY WITH STRATEGY 2

As we established in the graphical journey of the preceding pages, when it comes to teaching, some competencies signal Credibility way more than others do.

Consider two skills:

- the creation of visually appealing slides for the slide deck you use with students and
- the creation of a classroom environment where behavior is orderly and conducive to all students learning.

Which of these competencies is likely to send a stronger signal of Credibility to your students? While the slides definitely do send a signal, the sense that classroom behavioral dynamics are controlled sends a much stronger one. In a well-stewarded classroom, students and teacher alike can focus on the work of learning and need not be on edge awaiting the next swing in group behavior.

Our first step in Strategy 2, then, is to be sure that we're selecting an area of improvement that has the greatest chance to improve our Credibility signalling to students. I've identified eight areas that seem to come up again and again in my conversations with both students and teachers. Four of them can be practiced during instructional time, and four of them can be practiced outside of instructional time.

Areas to practice during instruction (these will have the most immediate effects on your Credibility):

- Classroom stewardship/management—that is, understanding the group psychology of the classroom and the methods that work best for creating a learning-conducive environment in which everyone feels heard, known, valued, and safe[14]

- Student motivation and engagement—that is, knowing how and why to cultivate the Five Key Beliefs in your classroom

- Basic, effective lesson preparation—that is, what lesson chunks work well in your course(s)? What kinds of activities can you use again and again for the sake of optimally advancing student mastery?[15]

- How students learn/the "science of learning"—that is, what are the core mechanics of the learning mind, and how do we create lessons and units that empower students to use and build their minds optimally?

Areas to practice outside of instruction (these will have more indirect but still important effects on your Credibility):

- Professional knowledge (content, pedagogy)—that is, pursuing a deep understanding of the content you are teaching and the ways students understand and misunderstand that content

- Teacher stress management—that is, knowing how to manage your life and stress amidst being an educator

- Working well with adults—that is, being a capable communicator and problem-solver with parents, guardians, colleagues, and bosses

- Teacher time management—that is, knowing how and when to apportion your time so that you get work done at work and have an easier time getting nights and weekends to yourself

---

[14]This is most often referred to by teachers in the United States as *classroom management*, but in many circles the term is out of favor. The term *stewardship* seems right to me for what we're after when we say classroom management. We're not seeking to be the rigid, lord-like bosses of our students; we're not seeking to micromanage young lives. Instead, we are seeking to be good managers— stewards—of a place and a people for whom we've been given a sacred trust.

[15]We'll examine this question further in Strategy 3: Gentle Urgency.

As you were reading through those, did any jump out at you or make you squirm? I recommend selecting an area that you seem intuitively drawn to or instinctively bothered by. These might be something that

- you can do well, but the way that you do it is very time- or energy-intensive and is therefore draining and nonsustainable;
- you cannot currently do well, despite trying; or
- you've up to this point in your career not prioritized.

Pick whatever area seems most likely to help you and your students.

Break Your Selected Area Down Into Its Subcomponents.

To avoid turning Strategy 2 into a reading slog, I'll treat the first two of the eight areas, dipsticking into considerations for each without fully unpacking either one of them. If you're interested in more in-depth takes on these areas, head to the companion website that I created for this book using the QR code below.

 Scan the QR code to read more about the eight areas of competence.

Classroom Stewardship/Management

The goal of classroom stewardship is to create an environment where students have the opportunity each day for an enjoyable, productive learning experience. This doesn't mean micromanaging behavior, but it does mean developing a keen handle on group behavioral dynamics.

In my experience, this begins with selecting, teaching, and reinforcing basic classroom rules. I know that many teachers seek to build lists of these with their students collaboratively, and I do not have any problems with that. In my own practice, I prefer to spend as little time talking about behavioral rules as possible, and so I come right out of the gate with the rules that I expect students to follow:

- Listen and follow directions.
- Raise your hand before speaking.
- Keep hands, feet, and objects to yourself.
- Respect one another.
- Use technology appropriately.

Those are it. I frame them on the first day by telling my students that my goal as their teacher is to create an environment where everyone can enjoy themselves and grow toward mastery. I tell them that, to me, this is like a precious and delicate treasure, and that I've found these rules are good and simple ways for all of us to protect that treasure.

The hand-raising rule can be tough for students to understand at times. After all, we don't raise our hands to speak in the cafeteria or around the dinner table, right? We won't do this in our jobs, will we? I explain it to them by saying that when you're in a larger group like we are,[16] hand-raising is a sensible way to avoid a small number of people dominating the air waves or a large number of people talking over one another.

As I write this, I'm sensitive to the fact that this all may sound overly procedural or controlling. This is the trouble with writing about classroom stewardship—it can sound like one thing and in reality feel like something entirely different. So, if you're concerned that my students are feeling controlled, I invite you to come visit my classroom and speak with them.

Another important subskill within classroom stewardship is a warmly authoritative teacher presence. What we're after here is signalling, with lots of unspoken signals, that we are people who know what we're doing. Our colleague Lynsay Fabio is a secondary ELA teacher in New Orleans, and to me she is the master of this move.[17] She breaks it down into what you do with your body, your voice, and your word choice.

---

[16]My class sizes most often range between thirty and thirty-five.

[17]Lynsay is the lead author on *The Classroom Management Course*, which you can get individual, group, or school access to at https://davestuartjr.com/CMC.

THINGS TO DO WITH YOUR BODY	THINGS TO DO WITH YOUR VOICE	THINGS TO DO WITH YOUR WORD CHOICE
Stand up straight, shoulders back. **Set your feet hips-width apart.** **Square up to whomever you're speaking to.** If speaking to the whole class, your body faces the whole class. If addressing one student, square up with that individual student. **Stand still.** Don't fidget or shift from foot to foot. **Relax your body parts.** Tension can be held in your fists, jaw, or even the spot between your eyebrows. Taking a deep breath helps. **Make eye contact.** When speaking to the whole class, dwell on an individual student's eyes for a few seconds, and then move to another. Lynsay notes that it's important not to be intimidating with this eye contact—you're not trying to stare anyone down or give the evil eye. Instead, you are trying to convey that you are unafraid and confident. **Smile.** Let the smile reach your eyes.	**Be loud.** Not obnoxiously so, but, in Lynsay's words, "much louder than most people tend to speak." This projects confidence, and it also ensures that all students can clearly hear you. **Be decisive.** Your voice should come down at the end of a sentence, not go up. **Don't end instructions with "Okay?"** This makes you sound unsure of the instruction you've just given. **Be emotionally neutral.** Don't betray anger or annoyance. "You want your voice to sound calm and controlled, without any emotional baggage." In my experience, this takes lots of practice—and then the even deeper skill of not being easily angered or annoyed takes loads more. **Speak slowly and with pauses.** Don't fall into the common nervousness trap of speaking faster than you need to.	**Keep it formal.** There are times for lowering our formality level with students within professional bounds (e.g., when greeting them in the hall), but moments of instruction are not those times. Also, note that formality isn't the same thing as coldness or lifelessness. I would describe Fred Rogers as pretty formal in his show, but he's certainly not cold or aloof. **Keep it concise.** When giving directions, don't use five sentences if only one will work. **Learn and use student names.** Few things ring in the heart like the sound of one's name on the lips of another. **Regularly say that it's a good feeling to be with your students.** Yes, this is straight from the playbook of the "Godfather of Warmth" himself, Mr. Fred Rogers.

An effective classroom steward also apprentices themselves to two kinds of teacher moves: those that help prevent misbehaviors and those that can be used when responding to them.

Moves that prevent misbehaviors include things like meeting students at the doorway at the start of class, assigning students' seats, regularly scanning the classroom to keep aware of what is happening, giving clear directions, and periodically updating students on how much time is left in a given learning segment. Many of these are overlooked by folks who struggle with stewarding classroom behavior.

For example, consider the giving of clear directions. It's shocking how frequently I've seen smart teachers give confusing directions. This almost always leads to student behaviors that are not conducive to learning. To remedy this, you've got to practice making your instructions for a given learning segment as *concise* as they can be. It also helps to *break instructions down into steps*. To reinforce directions, during the learning segment you want to be walking amongst students and clarifying your directions as needed. (This will also give you feedback on where you're being unclear.) With all of this, picture yourself as an athletic coach or musical tutor who is seeking to help your players grow and perform at their personal best.[18]

Sometimes, of course, students don't behave in ways that are optimally conducive to learning. In such cases, how does the credible teacher respond? Some methods—like raising your voice—are pretty bad for Credibility. Others, like those in the list that follow, tend to bolster Credibility.

- _____ I need _____: If a student is behaving in a manner not conducive to learning, it can be helpful to remind them with an impersonal "John, I need you to analyze these documents" or "Joanne, I need you to make a brave attempt at drawing a circle."
- Proximity: During direct instruction, I like to keep myself in the same place in the classroom that I always instruct from, but during independent or collaborative learning segments, it's best to circulate through the room. I tell early career

---

[18]Credit to my boss Todd Simmons for this phrase of "personal best."

teachers that if you haven't been within three feet of each of your students several times per lesson, you're likely missing something.

- Stop and examine: If you're giving instructions and a student begins engaging in behavior not conducive to learning (e.g., motioning to another student across the room), stop your instruction and stare (nonthreateningly!) at the student. The change in noise will often be enough to help the student redirect themselves.

- Nonverbals: Small gestures like a finger in the air, a finger to the lips, or a warm but steady gaze can help students redirect.

- One more time: If you shift into a learning mode (e.g., if in physical education class students are transitioning to a new part of the gym, or if in a biology lab students are collecting their lab materials) and you see five or more students not behaving in a manner conducive to learning, politely require students to try the transition one more time.

And finally, effectively stewarded classrooms tend to have well-defined, clearly taught, and consistently reinforced procedures for the things that happen repeatedly in the classroom. In my room, I teach students the procedure for entering the room, beginning the warm-up, talking in partners or groups, and coming back to attention after a collaborative learning segment.

Basic, Effective Lesson Preparation

Just as with classroom stewardship, basic and effective lesson preparation is most quickly mastered by breaking lessons down into their basic chunks. Different disciplines will look differently in this area, but I hope that in the following pages I can at least help you think clearly about the concept.

The goal with this area of competence is to think of your lesson planning in terms of blocks. What you want is to develop a repertoire of activities that work well in each of the blocks. This will allow you to speed up your lesson planning *and* get better faster at the activities you use again and again.

The first subcomponent of this skill is to identify the starter chunks that you can use. In my classroom, I call this the lesson

Credibility

Basic, Effective Lesson Anatomy

each block is proportional	**Warm-up**	• students working independently • teacher attempting an MGC • teacher completing admin tasks
	Lesson intro/ go over warm-up	• teacher or students provide lesson rationale • students share warm-up work • teacher gives whole-class feedback
lesson chunks = 12–15 minutes apiece	**Lesson chunk 1**	• students read or listen to a knowledge-rich text • teacher provides direct instruction and guided practice • teacher models how to put forth wise effort in learning
	Lesson chunk 2	• students read or listen to a knowledge-rich text • teacher provides direct instruction and guided practice • teacher models how to put forth wise effort in learning
	Lesson chunk 3	• students read or listen to a knowledge-rich text • teacher provides direct instruction and guided practice • teacher models how to put forth wise effort in learning
these smaller segments are about 3–6 minutes apiece	**Tie it all together**	• teacher leads reflective application of today's lesson • students make connections
	Closing	• teacher gives mini-sermon on value of lesson students engage in engaging retrieval practice (e.g., Quizlet, Kahoot, Gimkit, Blooket)

warm-up, while other teachers refer to it as a "bell ringer" or "do now" or "activate and engage." What matters is not what you call it; what matters is that you draw from as few learning activities as possible so that your students are accustomed to how lessons start in your room and what it looks like for them to attend optimally to those lesson beginnings.

Here are some examples from various disciplines:

- In physical education class, students may get dressed for class and follow the stretch leader in warm-ups.

- In science class, students may watch and discuss a brief YouTube clip about a recent scientific breakthrough.

- In history class, students may read and respond to a "This Day in History" article on the Internet, or they might read a blurb about a recent event and discuss how it connects to what they've been learning.

- In ELA, students may read independently at the start of class, or they may complete some mechanics warm-ups.

- In visual arts, students may complete a sixty-second sketch of what the teacher puts on the screen, or they may set an intention for the day's work time.

- In performing arts, students may view a brief performance and analyze it together.

- In band, students may tune their instruments or work through their scales.

The idea is to have as many types of warm-up chunk options as you absolutely need and then to teach, model, and reinforce for your students how to do these warm-ups with excellence as they begin their learning time in your room. And so on throughout the rest of the blocks.

What blocks of learning work well for facilitating learning during the middle of your lessons? Determine what modes of learning work best for your content area. Once you identify blocks that work for your discipline, you will find that your lesson planning (and the success of your lessons) becomes increasingly easy and effective. As you practice your different block types, think of yourself as an athlete or musician practicing; analyze how things go like one would a game or performance.

Then, what blocks work well to end your lessons? In what ways do learning sessions in your content area ideally end? What culture-enhancing blocks could you reliably incorporate into the end of some of your lessons?

Finally, what kinds of blocks work well when your lessons end up having extra time? I call these incidental or "time permitting" chunks. Every teacher needs a small bundle of moves they can use in the event of extra time at the end of a class period. These may be review games in a content area, quick challenges in phys ed, a list of short and fascinating YouTube videos, and so on.

And that's how this strategy works.

1. Take one of the eight core competency areas we've listed in this strategy that you think would make your life and your students' experiences in your class noticeably better.

2. Break the competency area down into its subcomponents so as to make it easier to practice and improve.

3. As needed, watch colleagues in action or read books on teaching to help your improvement along.

But always, always, always, remember: Improving at one thing at a time isn't settling for mediocrity. Instead, it's being smart with your labor and focus.

COMMON TEACHER HANG-UPS

I'm Bad at Everything—Help!

In the Stuart household, we would call this kind of language "catastrophizing." We'd smile at you with our whole faces and we'd say, "Hey now. Hey. Did you wear clothes to school today? Tie your shoes? Brush your teeth? Well, all right—then you're not bad at everything."

What you're feeling with this hang-up—and trust me, I've thought this very thing, said this very thing, *felt this very thing in my bones*—is that the ways in which you're incompetent are overwhelming and threatening. You are demoralized and burnt out. You're in the valley.

The only thing to do in these cases is just what we've said in this chapter: Pick one thing and for the next month allow everything else in your practice to maintain while you work relentlessly to improve this one area that you've chosen.

In many cases, teachers who are feeling bad at everything need to begin with classroom stewardship or lesson design. What skills and practices go into creating a learning environment that's enjoyable and productive for all? That's a mission-critical question, and neglecting to answer it means every lesson of every day will tend toward being not enjoyable and frustrating. Give yourself permission, this next quarter or so, to just answer that question, which I'll ask again: What skills and practices go into creating a learning environment that's enjoyable and productive for all?

My School's Asking Me to Do Things That Aren't on Your List.

Many well-meaning leadership teams craft professional development (PD) that may not align with the core competencies I've outlined above. We must empathize with the challenges our leaders face when preparing PD. They've got teachers at all kinds of experience and ability levels, and they receive input from all angles.

Even as we empathize, however, we must be mindful of the work that matters most for our own practice and in our own classrooms. I would never recommend that a teacher act adversarially with an administrator, but I do recommend that teachers set their inner focus on the prioritization that we've examined in this chapter. What that looks like, practically, is that if your administration is focusing a whole year of PD on, say, writing success criteria, you not overly stress yourself with this matter. Do the bare minimum—that is, satisfice it, don't skip it—and then save your heart and energy for the more critical work that you have identified.

(Continued)

(Continued)

This isn't to say that success criteria aren't important—they surely can be when they aid clarity in the classroom. Rather it is to say that in a classroom devoid of competency in basic classroom stewardship, even the best success criteria in the world won't do a whole lot of good.

First things first.

The biggest trouble with the advice I've given here is that many teachers feel uncomfortable satisficing anything that they are asked to do. "Good enough" is an anathematic way of thinking for them. Yet satisficing is one of the most well-worn tools in the belt of the teacher that flourishes in this work long term. I know of no way to do it sanely that does not include lots of "good enough" decisions in service of maximizing the few things that produce the greatest good for our students.

Strategy 3: Gentle Urgency

The idea here is that we want to signal from the start to the end of all of our class periods that what we're doing with students is of great importance. We want to embody the reality that every student in our room represents a *sacred trust*; their guardians send them to school expecting that they will learn and ultimately grow into people who can flourish long term.

Each moment of class is, in the sense of this sacred trust, inestimably precious. So there ought to be an urgency about us that our students can sense and that we often give voice to.

And yet—and yet!—many of our schools are toxically urgent at a systemic level. We obsess over whether students are "ahead" or "behind" or "on track," as if they are corporate projects that must meet deadlines.

So, as teachers, our sense of sacred urgency must be balanced by a palpable kindness, calm, peace, and gentleness. In our overpressured society, we must "teach with urgency but not to the point that it causes undue stress" (Fisher et al., 2020, p. 19).

What to Do

Start of Class	• Have a warm-up ready on the board while you complete admin tasks or one or two MGC attempts; practice this warm-up procedure with your students until it becomes secondhand.
Middle of Class	• Transition between learning activities thoughtfully and efficiently.
	• Simplify lesson materials so as to minimize wasted time or distractions.
	• Check for understanding frequently throughout the lesson, making judgments as you go on whether pacing needs more or less speed.
End of Class	• Have a small selection of end-of-lesson reinforcement or enrichment activities that can be used in the event that your plans end early.
Other Considerations	• Set and reinforce deadlines (with low-cost options for grace).
	• Promise your students that you will never assign busywork.
	• Practice your call to attention with students so that these critical moments in a lesson are peaceful for both you and them.
	• Remind students to work hard and enjoy the process.

How Strategy 3 Influences the Five Key Beliefs

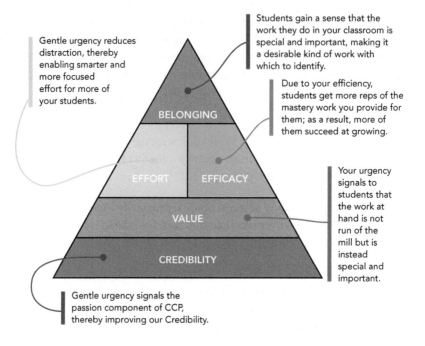

Gentle urgency reduces distraction, thereby enabling smarter and more focused effort for more of your students.

Students gain a sense that the work they do in your classroom is special and important, making it a desirable kind of work with which to identify.

Due to your efficiency, students get more reps of the mastery work you provide for them; as a result, more of them succeed at growing.

BELONGING

EFFORT

EFFICACY

VALUE

CREDIBILITY

Your urgency signals to students that the work at hand is not run of the mill but is instead special and important.

Gentle urgency signals the passion component of CCP, thereby improving our Credibility.

Gentle urgency is striking a balance. According to this concept, the time in our classrooms is precious—and therefore we're *urgent*—but because an education is a lifelong project, we're not in a hurried and breathless rush to arrive—and therefore we're *gentle*.

So, why aim for this?

I'll say it again: classroom time is a sacred trust. Many of us don't think about this enough—about all of the human beings who are behind the human beings that sit in our classrooms each day. Take Student One on your roster, for example—as we've said, she's a universe all her own, but so are all of her parents and guardians and coaches and grandparents and friends who hope for her well-being. As we seek to help Student One to grow in mastery of our subjects, we're doing it as people implicitly trusted with Student One's long-term flourishing. And so indeed, as professor Clyde Kilby once wrote, "Today, this very day, some stroke is being added to the cosmic canvas" (Piper, 2013, p. 198). It's not just Day Ten on the countdown to winter break; it's the only December 5, 2022, that this student will ever have.

There's a gentle but profound *urgency* in that.

Second, gentle urgency is an aid to your own long-term flourishing in this work. If you teach lessons as if time is something to be gotten through, as if the clock is a thing to burn, then it should come as no surprise that you eventually find yourself not eager to return to work in the morning, lackluster to face another day. Strategy 3 helps you to practice the reality that we've just described: that you've been given a precious thing in today's lesson and that you, more than anyone else in the room, ought to represent and make known that inherent preciousness. This will give you a sense of purpose that will make the passion component of Credibility's CCP stand out all the brighter in you.

HOW TO GAIN PROFICIENCY WITH STRATEGY 3

At all times, think on the tension between gentle and urgent. Much of the power of Strategy 3 is contained in the nuance of its title. Let's use a small table to illustrate:

GENTLE	URGENT
I greet students with a smile and I think about that smile expanding all the way up into my eyes.	I exhort students to get right to the warm-up; I teach and reinforce our warm-up procedure every day for a month so that we're getting right into learning as soon as the bell rings.
I teach my students that one part of success in high school is growing academically. I remind them of this often and paint it to be a worthy and timeless endeavor.	I teach my students that another part of success in high school is enjoying the process. I often say, "If you become valedictorian of your class at the cost of four years of being miserable and stressed, no one has missed the mark on high school so much as you."

As we explored a bit on pages 85–88, I like to think of lessons in terms of blocks of learning activity. In this strategy I'd like to help you focus on weaving gentle urgency into these lesson blocks.

Start of Class

In a gently urgent classroom, students have something important to do the minute that class begins. In my room, this is almost always a written warm-up of some kind. These may be short-answer question prompts that review previously learned content (see Strategy 5: Feast of Knowledge), or they may be prompts inviting students to set a goal (see Strategy 8: Define Success) or reflect on how a recent unit went (see Strategy 9: Unpack Outcomes, Good or Bad).

To aid in urgency, be sure to teach your students what you expect during these class warm-ups. In my room, I expect students to do the following:

- Have a seat, read the warm-up slide, and begin work right away.

- Follow directions in a manner that respects their fellow students' need to focus and learn (e.g., except in rare cases, the warm-up will require independent writing and therefore students should remain quiet and work independently).

In our colleague Justin Harnden's TV production class, students sometimes begin class by writing quick narratives or storylines; in his theater classes, students sometimes construct character bios.

To aid in gentleness, these methods help:

- When speaking about this start-of-class procedure, I explain to students that my goal is to provide them every day with an enjoyable and productive learning experience. That begins with a quiet and peaceful warm-up.

- While my students are engaged in the warm-up, I attend to quick administrative matters (e.g., taking attendance) and attempt an MGC or two. As I'm doing this, I remind myself to smile and let the smile reach my eyes.

Middle of Class

During your two or three learning segments within a lesson, gentle urgency is aided via the following means.

To aid in urgency, I try to

- teach my students how to transition between our various learning tasks (e.g., from independent writing to whole-class reading, or from article analysis to Think-Pair-Share) and practice these transitions until we've become proficient and

- think ahead about materials needed for the various activities I have planned, asking myself, "How could we do this with fewer materials? How might this become simpler?"

To aid in gentleness in the middle of the lesson, I try to

- remind my students *why* we practice efficient transitions (e.g., because learning is so good, our time together is so precious, and/or the chance to do all this is so enjoyable).

End of Class

It is common for secondary students to be eager to move on to the next class before your own class has ended. This looks like packing up materials early or queuing at the door.

To aid in urgency, I try to have a handful of "one last thing" exercises that my students and I can complete so as not to squander our last minutes together. These include the following:

- a tech-aided retrieval practice activity (e.g., Quizlet, Kahoot, or Blooket) which aids with digesting the feast of knowledge we've enjoyed together (see Strategy 5)

- a "What I learned today" three-sentence reflection on Canvas

- a whole-class read-aloud of History.com's "This Day in History" article for the day

To aid in gentleness, consider these methods:

- I sometimes ask my students, "Hey, does anyone have something they're looking forward to tonight?"

- My principal Todd Simmons once ended a staff meeting with an Appreciation, Apology, Aha; anyone could share one or more of these things, and Mr. Simmons began by modeling one of each. It was an effective way to close our time.

- Wish your students well with something short and sweet. I like to say things like, "Be safe," or, "It was great being with you all today," or "You all take care now."

Other Tips for Gentle Urgency

- Be gentle with yourself, too. I know that sounds trite, but I've spoken to enough colleagues over the years to say with confidence that few professions are as filled with self-critics as teaching. My transitions in class aren't robotically perfect; my students don't always begin the warm-up as I'd like. What makes me a great teacher isn't some unrealistic level of perfection. Instead, it's that I care about my students, my craft, and my discipline.

- The most important during-class procedure for gentle urgency is, to me, the call-to-attention. This move allows you and your class to shift between two critical learning modes: quiet attention to a single speaker and active conversation amongst students.

- Take the time that you save lesson planning and invest it in other Strategy 2 areas. Because the building-block lesson planning method is so simple, you end up having more time to work on things that will make your building blocks great (e.g., research, collegial collaboration).

- Set and hold to deadlines for student work, but provide them with a low-cost means for grace. In my school, many teachers give students five emergency passes each semester that they can use for submitting assignments after deadlines. I find this to be a great gentle-urgency balancing technique: Deadlines still matter, but there's also a tool that can be used in the event that life happens and a deadline gets missed.

- Model gentle-urgent value sets. In my room I like to emphasize to students that we are learning to work hard *and* to enjoy the process. It's not just the urgency of hard work; it's also the gentleness of enjoyment.

- Promise your students that you'll never assign busywork. Your objective is their growth in mastery, and as a result there is no sense in giving them anything to do that's unrelated to that. This doesn't mean you don't use drills (I do, very intentional ones) and it doesn't mean there's never a printed sheet for students to work on. It just means that everything—*every thing*—that you assign is aimed at the advancement of your students' knowledge and skill in your discipline or art. Tell them that, and then live up to the promise. I invite my students to tell me when they perceive of something as busywork. If I cannot look myself in the mirror and give an honest, intelligent rationale for what they arc complaining about, I get rid of the assignment.

COMMON TEACHER HANG-UPS

It's Hard to Feel Urgent When I Don't Think What I Teach Is Important.

Genuine gentle urgency flows from an inner conviction that what we're doing with students *really* matters. And so, if you're teaching something that feels unimportant or unworthy of your students' time, how are you supposed to be gently urgent with your students?

I run into this myself from time to time. Here are the kinds of things I do that help most.

- **First, sit down by yourself with a blank sheet of paper and brainstorm ten reasons why what you're teaching could be important.** Early on in my tenure as an English 9 teacher, I had to do this when teaching Bradbury's *Fahrenheit 451.*

(Continued)

(Continued)

For the full story on my now-infamous Bradbury dilemma, scan the QR code.

This exercise helped me to see that, although Bradbury's writing was sometimes ill-suited to my fancy, it did nonetheless provide rich soil for student growth and great classroom discussions.

- **Next, share with your students the dilemma.** This has to be done carefully so as not to denigrate yourself, your discipline, or the folks who make curriculum decisions in your setting. One junior high physical education teacher in Utah does this by saying, "Class, tonight we have parent-teacher conferences, and I often have parents attend who tell me that physical education is not important and that their child doesn't need it. What kinds of things do you think I could say to parents who have a hard time valuing phys ed?" This places students in the position of both expert *and* arguer—a master move for engaging adolescents. And often I learn ways of thinking about what I'm teaching that I otherwise would not have.

- **Next, try rushing through the unimportant stuff and supplementing it with something that is important.** In one of my earliest teaching placements, I was given a scripted curriculum to work through with my middle schoolers. The students and I both found it insulting. To resolve this we devised a daily routine of rushing through the scripted work and giving ourselves time to read and workshop plays, novels, and poems.

- **Finally, it may be that you're right.** If you earnestly attempt to find value in what you're teaching and to enlist your students in this work, but the value still is not apparent, it may be time to request a different placement or seek a different school. This sounds extreme, but I don't think that it is. Few things are as harmful to a human soul as coercing that human into doing something that they know to be devoid of value. I hear from teachers who are asked to do things with students that I could not imagine myself doing without becoming a shadow of who I am today. I'm talking about hours of test prep exercises per day or hopelessly watered down and incoherent curricula. If none of the above strategies are helping you, it may be time to find a new place.

Value

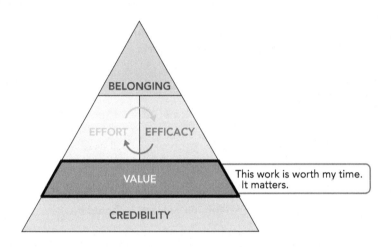

This work is worth my time. It matters.

BELONGING

EFFORT | EFFICACY

VALUE

CREDIBILITY

WHAT IT IS

WHAT **VALUE** SOUNDS LIKE	WHAT **ANTI-VALUE** SOUNDS LIKE
Science is important.	Science is dumb.
Math is going to make me better at life.	Math doesn't help you in life, especially the kind of math we do in Painter's class.
Reading makes me happy.	Reading is for nerds.
Writing is a skill I can use in almost any profession.	Writing is useless and dumb.
History is challenging and intriguing.	History is annoying.
The skills I'm learning in woodworking will be useful my whole life.	Woodworking is lame.
I'm going to use Spanish when I live in _____.	I'm never going to use dumb Spanish.

When students don't optimally value school, they'll say things like this:

- "This is boring."
- "This is pointless."
- "Why do we have to do this?"
- "When will I ever use this in my life?"

When they don't optimally value an assignment, you'll know by sounds like this when you introduce the work:

- "Awww man!"
- "Really!?!"
- "Whyyyyyyy?!"
- "Ughghghgh!"

Here's why: Your classroom is an alternate world from the one your students normally inhabit. Or at least, it should be.

It's a *cosmos*—Latinized from the Greek *kosmos*: a good order, an orderly arrangement; *a world.*

Whether you teach art or agriculture, social studies or Scripture, English language arts or personal finance, you are, day by day, through helping your students toward mastery of your discipline, inviting them into a cosmos.

And that, of course, means a bit of discomfort. It means work. It means sacrifice and movement. It means sometimes doing things that, at least initially, will make you make "Urrrghghgh!" noises.

LAUNDRY WORK

What's laundry like in your classroom?

I'm talking about those kinds of learning assignments that *need* to be done for the optimal growth of your students but that at the same time are kind of . . .

I'm afraid to say it, but . . .

Boring.

Mundane.

Run of the mill.

Not flashy.

I'm talking about the things that, when you ask students to do them, you're likely to see eyes rolling or hear a chorus of "Do we haaaaaaaave to?"

I've asked a few thousand teachers this over the years in my workshops, and this table lists the kinds of things that I hear.

DISCIPLINE	LAUNDRY ASSIGNMENT
General	• Completing a tutorial request form • Taking notes on something they've read or watched • Having to use complete sentences and supporting their answers • Essay writing • Taking notes by hand
Phys ed	• Stretching
Literature	• Reading *Julius Caesar*
Writing	• Pre-writing • Proofreading
World history	• Reading and responding to a current events article every week • Writing an essay response to a document-based question
U.S. history	• Annotating a text
Government	• Memorizing the Amendments • Mandatory public speaking assignments
Algebra I	• Setting up a problem before beginning to solve it
Algebra II	• Completing practice problems
Geometry	• Explaining the solution method used for a problem

(Continued)

(Continued)

DISCIPLINE	LAUNDRY ASSIGNMENT
Biology	• Writing a lab report • Taking notes
Chemistry	• Memorizing twenty-five polyatomic ions • Solving stoichiometric equations
Welding	• Completing a project with wasted metal
Foods and nutrition	• Writing and reading a recipe before they cook
Drawing	• Learning how to draw shapes and turn them into more complex drawings
Painting	• Painting a still life
Theater	• Memorizing a script
TV production	• Scripting a news segment
Marching band	• Practicing their instrument • Learning scales and arpeggios
Symphonic band	• Warm-ups and exercises
Computer science	• Debugging a program
Language (e.g., Spanish, French)	• Memorizing vocabulary words
Personal finance	• Writing a budget
A boarding school I once visited in Mt. Calvary, Wisconsin	• Doing actual laundry

We've all got laundry assignments, don't we? Growing in mastery toward anything is typically going to require some laundry. Thinking about these assignments helps us to understand the challenge and the opportunity of the Value belief. When our students ask, with their mouths or with their hearts, why we are doing an activity, what they are revealing to us is a struggle with Value.

THE RAINBOW OF WHY

The core graphic for my thinking on the Value belief is a lovely painter's palette called the Rainbow of Why.[19]

---

[19]All props to our colleague Doug Anderson for that language—when I was showing this image to his faculty using the heading Value Palette, Doug instead called it the Rainbow of Why. The name stuck!

the **RAINBOW** of **WHY**

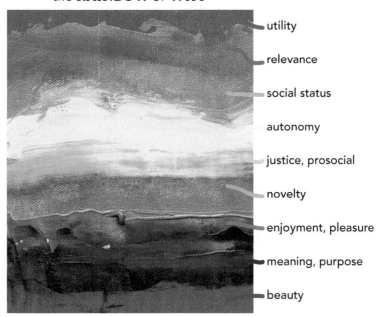

- utility
- relevance
- social status
- autonomy
- justice, prosocial
- novelty
- enjoyment, pleasure
- meaning, purpose
- beauty

pexels.com/Steve Johnson

Value

Key Understanding 1: The Rainbow of Why Is Good News.

I love this image for several reasons:

- In its colorfulness, it communicates beauty, playfulness, and hope. That's exactly how I want you to think about cultivating Value. You're not trying to strong-arm your students into valuing what you do; you're inviting them into a world of color and wonder.

- In its paintedness, it suggests creation, art, and innovation. Too often in education we talk about motivating students as if it's a chore. Instead, cultivating the Five Key Beliefs is a privilege and a pleasure. No matter what you teach, the wonderful thing is that your subject is good and worthy because education is good and worthy. All of your students can benefit. And so you need not groan beneath the weight of cultivating Value; you need only to get out your paints and play.

Key Understanding 2: American Secondary Schools Rely Too Heavily on Utility and Relevance; This Imbalance Harms the Hearts of Our Students.

Let's explain what I mean by utility and relevance in the graphic, and then I'll explain the shortcoming of relying too much on either in school.

Utility

Utility is usefulness. It answers the question, "When will I ever *use* what I'm learning right now?" It's one of two hues in the Rainbow of Why that American secondary schools tend to harmfully overuse.

What utility sounds like in a young person:

- "I'll use fractions when I bake cakes."
- "I'll use grammar and mechanics in my career as a writer."
- "I'll use strength training in physical education class during soccer season."

The key troubles in overusing utility:

I've asked over a thousand teachers across the United States to share with me their favorite answers to the timeless student question: "But *why* do we have to do *this*, teacher?" Well above 80 percent of educators answer these *why* questions with something to do with utility: "You'll *use* this when you _____." There are at least two problems with so many of us defaulting to utility explanations.

- First, they don't work all that well, especially when we make utility arguments about the future: "People discount the value of temporally distant rewards to an extreme and irrational degree" (Bryan et al., 2016). In other words, leaning on utility in math class —"Dave, you'll use this geometry someday if you're ever building a shed"—is like telling me that exercise or a diet will help me live healthier in twenty years. Living healthy longer is a temporally distant reward; it sounds great, but not *nearly* as great as another slice of pizza with ranch on the side—and that's coming from a

Value

middle-aged man. Teenagers have an even harder time valuing things that are temporally distant.

- Second, when we overuse utility, I think we send a motivationally deadly unspoken message. This message is, if you can't use what you're learning in school then there's no point in learning it. Which leads to wonderings like, "Wait—my teacher cannot say when I'll use this today? Ha—I got 'em! Time for me to sit back and relax." Over a hundred years ago, edu-philosopher Mason (2017 [reprint]) basically called this when she warned against using too few methods for motivating young people lest we call one set of motives "unduly into play to the injury of the child's character" (p. 141). It's that last part —"injury of the child's character"—that I find so haunting as I look into the eyes of a student that demands to know when today's lesson will be used.

The key solution to our overuse of utility:

Now, far be it from me to bring up a problem without proposing the silver lining. Here's how I think we overcome a culture obsessed with utility.

Teach that no adult knows just what they know from their K-12 education. I had a lovely, talented, and hard-working eighth-grade science teacher, Mrs. Lavoie. She was just fantastic. But believe it or not, when I try remembering things from her class as a middle-aged man today, I can call to mind just two things: a picture of a food web, and her warm smiling face.

So does this mean that Mrs. Lavoie taught me nothing that I use today? That the 180 or so hours I spent in her science class were wasted? Heavens no! What a silly and unsacred thought. Yet this is just what some adults seem to think when they get up on TED stages and rail against how the industrial model of education is ruining lives today.

The reality is that during the reading of these past three paragraphs, your mind has been transformed. Your neuropathways are just a bit different. If I were to ask you to think in exactly the same way this evening as you thought this morning, it would not be possible. Why? Because due to your neuroplasticity you are a creature ever changing.

With that said, teach your students that their educational time is precious and deserves never to be wasted. In the spirit of Strategy 3's gentle urgency, I want my students to know that it's important to me that our class time is always wisely invested. I have no tolerance for things like busywork—activities meant to keep kids occupied and placid. Instead, we are obsessed with moving toward mastery in our discipline. "We are not about busywork," I often say to my students.

And that, dear colleague, is something that will never waste your time and will always enrich your life. These are the kinds of things we must say *relentlessly* to repair student hearts that have been malformed by utilitarianism.

Relevance

Relevance is relatability. It's, "How does this lesson connect with my interests, values, hobbies, and goals?"

What relevance sounds like in a young person:

- "I'm interested in being a YouTuber, so this video editing unit in my TV production elective is useful to me."
- "I plan to have children someday, so this family science lesson on infant-rearing is important to me."
- "I like writing songs to play on my guitar at home, so when we analyzed those Taylor Swift lyrics in English class, I resonated with that."

The key troubles in overusing relevance:

The biggest problem I see in teachers who rely too much on relevance is that they presume that student interests are more homogenous than they actually are. For example, in a blog article I once read but will not cite out of respect for the author, the topic was culturally relevant pedagogy. Now mind you, I have a deep respect for CRP, having matriculated at an undergraduate program that was shaped around Ladson-Billings's (2001) *Crossing Over to Canaan*. I believe all good teaching is culturally responsive.

In the article I'm referencing, the author provided an exemplar lesson in which students were asked to analyze a Taylor Swift song rather than an Emily Dickenson poem. The Taylor Swift song, the author implied, was relevant to student cultures in a way that the Dickenson poem was not.

This is deeply problematic to me as a Five Key Beliefs practitioner for the following reasons:

- On the one hand, the student who has total interest in Taylor Swift—a Swiftie through and through—has now received a signal that *only* optimally relevant things are worth studying in school. In the long-term, signals like this undermine the Value belief because not *every* lesson of *every* discipline can be optimally aligned to one's individual preferences.
- On the other hand, the students who have zero interest in Taylor Swift—anti-Swifties, let's call them—have now received an anti-Belonging signal that their identities are at odds with the kind of work done in their English class.
- And, for this latter group, the teacher's Credibility has likely diminished because the teacher seems to care more about Swifties than about anti-Swifties.

My point is to critique the popular narrative amongst American educators that relevant curricula are a simple and self-evident good. First of all, there is no classroom in the United States where relevance is simple. Our students are too diverse, their identities too complex. And second, in an Internet-saturated culture like the one we teach in, is an individually relevant education truly the best possible good we can provide for our students? I say let the algorithms master individualization; let's focus in school on mastering the disciplines.

The key solution to our overuse of relevance:

Basically, teach a broadly representative curricula that showcases the breadth and depth of your discipline. Dr. Bishop (1990) so aptly called for "mirrors and windows" in the curriculum: learning experiences that *reflect* your students, that are relevant to them; and learning experiences that *show* your students other worlds.

In other words: Just do the darn Dickenson poem! *And* do a song from pop culture once in a while. It's important for your students to experience the fullness of what your discipline or art offers, and that means giving them lots of chances to experience all the breadth and depth of what you teach.

Key Understanding 3: To Remedy Our Overreliance on Relevance and Utility, We've Got to "Paint" Intentionally With All the Other Colors of the Rainbow of Why.

Let's examine the other colors on the Rainbow of Why.

Social Status

Social status is our sense of how we measure up to others. It answers questions like, "What's my ranking? How does this activity affect my ranking? Am I more or less prestigious amongst my peers because of this thing?"

What social status sounds like in a young person:

- "My debate speech in civics class today was so much fun—all of my friends applauded."
- "I can't wait until the bake-off in food and nutrition class next month—it's going to be fun to compete with my peers."
- "I love playing Kahoot in science class. It's so intense to compete."
- "If there's not a competition involved in a classroom, I'll probably not be interested."

Key drawback:

Competition in class is a tricky thing—so much so that I'll treat it at length at the end of this chapter (see pages 118–120).

Autonomy

Adolescents are hypersensitive to being autonomous. They want control of their lives and the independence to make their own choices.

What autonomy sounds like in the heart of a young person:

- "I'm learning personal finance so I can save up for a car."

- "I like how in English class we get to choose our own books for independent reading."

- "Ms. Smith's a great agricultural science teacher because she lets us pick from several options for showing our mastery in each unit."

- "I'm paying attention in history so that I can have an informed discussion with my dad about politics."

From the research:

Providing autonomy for students doesn't require a major curricular overhaul. In one study, framing a request in terms of what one "should" do versus what one "might consider" prevented adolescents from internalizing a message or changing their behavior (Bryan et al., 2016). The latter's added sense of autonomy made a difference. One tiny language shift; big shift in perceived Value.

Justice, Prosocial

Justice is righting wrongs in the world. It's resisting what is evil or unfair. It's standing up for the oppressed. It's the pursuit of rightness.

Prosocial behavior is psychologese for something smaller than justice—think of it as the simple act of helping another. Though less dramatic than justice, it's still deeply good. Raising money for someone who has lost their home is prosocial; stopping to help a peer in the hallway who has dropped their belongings is prosocial.

What justice/prosocial sounds like in a young person:

- "I'm into this research paper that we're writing in English class because my topic is something that I believe is important and needs to improve in the world."

- "I enjoy earth science because I'm learning more about the environment and how it can be positively or negatively affected by my choices."

- "I like what we're studying in health because I'm learning to see the manipulative practices of food companies and how they encourage poor eating choices."

- "Personal finance is teaching me how to 'stick it to the man' by resisting consumer spending urges and saving a bit from each paycheck."

From the research:

It turns out that justice and/or prosocial angles can be especially appealing to adolescents. Bryan et al. (2016) demonstrated with a 536-student study that students were more likely to eat healthy foods when taught about the manipulative and unfair practices of the food industry (e.g., engineering junk food to be addictive and marketing it to young children) versus just being taught about unhealthy and healthy eating.

Value

Novelty

Novelty is when something's new. You're not used to it—in a good way. Its newness makes it interesting.

What novelty can look like in a classroom:

- Referring to your discipline in a way students are not used to (e.g., in Caroline Ong's example on page 128, she says, "Mathematicians are lazy!")
- Using a new review game in Spanish class
- Starting a new unit in computer science
- Starting a new book in ELA

Often overlooked point:

Novelty can come from things as small as the language you use or the way that your classroom makes every student feel like they are somebody. In other words, novelty need not come from constantly coming up with new lesson blocks.

Enjoyment, Pleasure

Enjoyment is fun. It's what we typically associate with being happy or entertained. It's the source of hedonic pleasure—a counterpart to the eudaimonic pleasure that we'll see in a moment.

What enjoyment sounds like in a young person:

- "It's fun answering the problems in the math textbook because they are just the right amount of challenging for me and I usually get them right."
- "I always look forward to pop-up debates because I know someone will say something funny and we'll all laugh."
- "My psychology teacher is really good at his job; he always makes learning fun."

Key idea:

The master play here is helping students broaden their sense of what is enjoyable and pleasurable. Just like beauty, enjoyment and pleasure are subjective. They are changeable, expandable states that can be influenced; we're not born with a fixed set of things we'll find fun and things we won't. So what you're after is helping your students to find joy and pleasure in the challenge of learning, in things that are not normally enjoyed by folks like them.

One great teacher move, then, is to expand your own sense of what is enjoyable and fun. Every half year or so I try enjoying the pursuit of a new hobby, the learning of a new topic, the cooking of a new food, or the enjoyment of a new kind of music.

Meaning, Purpose

Meaning is significance beyond the self. It's being caught up in something bigger than you and your life. It's the source of what philosophers call eudaimonic pleasure. It's what management thinker Sinek (2009) is talking about in his popular TED-talk-turned-book, *Start With Why*.

Purpose is a sense of what you're here for. It's the impact you'd like to have in the world. It's the thing about which you'd like to look back upon at the end of your life and say, "I accomplished that. I lived up to that."

What meaning and purpose sound like in a young person:

- "I'm going to become a nurse one day because I love to help people. Because of that, I care about what we're learning in our anatomy class. It aligns with my purpose."

- "When I read the end of the novel for English class last night, I couldn't describe the emotions within me. It felt good, and sad, and terrible, and beautiful."
- "Art brings people joy. This is why I love to make and share my art."
- "I want to serve my country as a marine one day, and so I'm all in when it comes to physical education class."
- "My mom had breast cancer when she was thirty, and so what we're studying in health class is especially significant for me."

From the research:

Psychologists are especially interested in eudaimonic pleasures such as meaning and purpose because they are associated with lots of beneficial side effects. For example, "The presence of meaning in an adolescents' life is associated with a host of positive indices of well-being, including higher self-esteem, higher happiness, lower distress, lower anxiety, and greater academic motivation" (Telzer et al., 2014, p. 6,601).

Key benefit:

Cultivating a sense of meaning and purpose in the work of learning is one of the best gifts that you can grant a young person. Meaning and purpose are nuclear fusion reactors of the Value belief; they form a foundation for a flourishing life.

Beauty

Beauty appeals to the aesthetic senses. It is deeply subjective and deeply influenced by context. One person can sit outside in a quiet park, listening to the wind through the trees, and be deeply moved by the beauty of the moment. A person sitting next to them, meanwhile, can be completely bored.

What beauty sounds like in a young person:

- "When my peer gave a presentation in science class today, I was moved by how well she spoke."
- "In physical education class, we watched an interview of a paraplegic who goes to the gym each day for exercise. I kept

thinking about it all day—not because I felt sorry for the person but because their attitude was beautiful."

- "In our ethnic studies elective, we got to read interviews from Holocaust survivors; though all were sad, some of them were beautiful in the hope I read between the lines."

Key benefit:

Despite its subjectivity, a strong sense for beauty in school is nothing short of a superpower. When a student learns to see beauty in the everyday (e.g., in Caroline Ong's class, where the beauty of math is spoken of often; see pages 127–129), that student will have little trouble valuing school.

Key Understanding 4: It Helps to Represent Learning in Lots of Ways.

Here's a multiple choice question that can really teach us something:

Learning is _____.

    A. when I take in new information

    B. about remembering, using, and ultimately understanding information

    C. difficult but important

    D. about improving as a person and widening my perspective

    E. a process that takes place every day of our lives

    F. not only studying at school but also knowing how to be considerate to others

How would you answer that? I'll leave a few blank spaces here so you can answer it without being tempted by the "correct answer."

Got your answer?

The above options are taken from a tool created by Nola Purdie and John Hattie to measure student conceptions of learning. The tool makes several dozen statements (six of which I just shared), and those statements can be grouped into the following clusters, which I'll line up with our options above.

A. learning as gaining information

B. learning as remembering, using, and understanding information

C. learning as duty

D. learning as personal change

E. learning as process

F. learning as social competence

Interestingly, I find that teachers (myself included) tend to operate using (or at least communicating) just a few of the above conceptions of learning. Our defaults are narrower than the list above. Which seems fine, right? Until you see what Purdie and Hattie discovered when they compared the quantity of conceptions of learning a student held with that student's achievement. Fascinatingly, it wasn't any one conception that gave students an achievement advantage. *The more conceptions they had, the better they tended to do in school.*

In other words, the "correct answer" to our multiple choice question is, at least when it comes to student achievement, all of the above. I don't know why that is, but my guess is that a student with such a broad array of outlooks has an easier time engaging with any learning task they're presented with.

This is fascinating because, at least in my experience, teachers tend to assume that their philosophy of learning is the right one: "*Everyone knows* learning is __." Progressive teachers are certain that learning is about the process of personal or societal change, and they generally flinch when learning is considered a duty or simply about information. On the other hand, traditionalists get frustrated when learning is presented as a social-emotional process or a personal journey; they focus on building knowledge and the importance of this for a well-functioning democratic society.

But, according to Purdie and Hattie, both the progressives and the traditionalists are only partially right. The most productive view of learning is one that encompasses all of their views. So how do we help kids build a full spectrum of conceptions of learning?

It's likely that the most robust method for broadening our students' conceptions of learning is contextual rather than interventional; creating classrooms in which all of the conceptions are reinforced by learning tasks. Practically, this means using the conceptions as a filter through which to view our lessons and assignments. In *X* lesson or *Y* assignment, what conception of learning am I reinforcing? Let's examine this using two sample assignments from my classes this year.

Sample Assignment 1: Memorizing Dozens of Dates in World History.

I can communicate this assignment through several of the conceptions of learning. First, it is about acquiring information. But, more importantly and strategically, it is about remembering, using, and understanding the information gained for a long time. Also, this assignment is difficult and certainly not always fun; that's learning as duty. Yet when the work is through and kids are recognizing dates they've memorized in texts, videos, conversations, and movies, and as they begin to make use of an ever-accessible timeline that doesn't require Wi-Fi, they start seeing themselves differently and being proud of their improvement (learning as personal change).

The way in which I talk about this assignment and the ways in which I lead students to approach it and converse about it and reflect on it—these are the moves that help develop more diverse conceptions of learning.

Sample Assignment 2: Reading a Novel (*Things Fall Apart*) in World History.

Chinua Achebe's novel isn't part of our school's mandated world history curriculum, which forces me to move quickly through the mandated units so that we have time for *Things Fall Apart* at the end of fall semester. I regularly tell my kids that we work harder than the mandated curriculum requires so that we can work even harder at reading a great (but challenging) novel, and I try to frame that motivationally by communicating the following:

- We are a group that does hard things, including working hard at learning (learning as duty).

- This hard work makes us develop as people, and reading *Things Fall Apart* will broaden our horizons (learning as personal change).

- *Things Fall Apart* will enable us to take a location-specific look at the effects of imperialism on one African society (gaining information), and this will in turn help us understand imperialism at a greater level than we would if we were not to read it.

- *Things Fall Apart* will also lead us to consider what it means to be masculine or feminine, and this ought to help us better relate to ourselves on a day-to-day basis (learning as process) and to others (learning as social competence).

The Big Idea for Us as Teachers

The big idea for me is that I want to internalize each of these conceptions of learning—I want to memorize them and use them—so that I communicate them all throughout the year. This, I hope, will help me build more lessons and assignments that engender the full spectrum of conceptions in my kids. In light of Purdie and Hattie's research, I can no longer afford to emphasize solely the conceptions I'm drawn to; I need to communicate them all.

Value, it turns out, is less about what learning *is* than it is about why learning *matters*. But the Hattie/Purdie study is a useful complement to this idea of painting with all the colors of the Rainbow of Why.

COMMON TEACHER HANG-UPS

My Students Only Seem to Be Motivated When There's a Competition Involved.

Competition is tricky because some people *really* like it and some people really *don't*. When competition comes up in my teacher workshops as a source of Value for students, I like to ask the room two questions. First, I ask students to raise their hands if they *love* competition, and then I ask them to raise their hands if they *loathe* competition. Hands always go up for both questions. And so, what are we to do as teachers who want all of our students to have productive and enjoyable learning experiences in our classrooms?

I think that part of the answer is found in the Rainbow of Why. When we think of a classroom competition—say, a game of Quizlet or Kahoot on the mild end, or a March Madness–style bracket debate on the other—a few facets of the rainbow are in play.

the **RAINBOW** of **WHY**

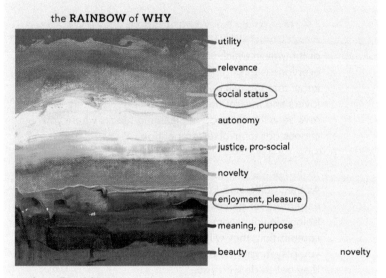

- utility
- relevance
- social status
- autonomy
- justice, pro-social
- novelty
- enjoyment, pleasure
- meaning, purpose
- beauty   novelty

pexels.com/Steve Johnson

- Social status: "If I win, I move up! But if I lose, I move down." Some students may not enjoy competition because they don't need social status to be a motivator in a given course; for example, they may find history fascinating on its own terms without incorporating a game, and so a competition feels like a needless risk. Whereas competition lovers may find history boring and therefore the chance to rise in social status is highly appealing.

  o Another trouble with the social status draw is that students who could potentially be motivated by an improvement in social status during a game you're playing may view themselves as so incapable of winning (an Effort/Efficacy issue) that they completely stop trying.

(Continued)

Value

(Continued)

- Enjoyment, pleasure: Some students are socially and emotionally mature enough to compete in games without deep concern for who wins or loses; they simply enjoy the different mode of learning.

So, what are we to do? I see a few opportunities.

- Ask your students my two questions above: Who loves competition? Who hates it? Emphasize to them that part of the way in which you'll create a room of challenge for everyone is through occasional competitive events. You know that this will be motivating for the competition lovers and frustrating for the competition haters, but the reverse will be true during learning blocks where you choose not to involve competition.

- The rest of the strategies outlined in this book will help make competitions safer in your classroom for students. As their ability and Efficacy improve, so too will their eagerness for games. As they come to believe that they belong in your room no matter the outcome of some competition, they will be more likely to find the games you play in your class another important part of the work they get to do with you.

My Students Only Care About Grades.

Most teachers I speak with nod their heads when I describe grade-mongering—that is, when a student is only willing to do course work that is graded. A *monger* is a dealer or trader; for example, a fishmonger deals or trades only in fish. And a grade-monger is someone who deals or trades only in grades. Like all of our students, those caught up in grade-mongering are good people.

Grade-mongering, however, is a massive obstacle to proper motivation in our secondary schools. Refer back to the purpose of school that we covered at the beginning of this book: Schools exist to promote the long-term flourishing of young people, specifically by teaching them to master the disciplines and arts. Where in that definition have I included grades?

Now, let me be clear: I'm not a "get rid of grades" guy. But in my own practice and research, I don't find a fixation on grading systems to be necessary for helping my students to move their hearts away from grade-mongering and toward a mastery orientation.

The main thing that I find helps is that I keep my grading system as simple as possible. I don't have complete autonomy over this—for example, my department decides on the 60/40 summative/formative weighting split that we use for our marking period grades—but wherever I do have autonomy, such as in deciding what to grade as formative and how to grade things that are formative, I lean heavily toward simplicity.

Let me expand on my grading practices, as I am often asked questions about them.

- Although I require students to complete a daily written warm-up, I rarely if ever grade this. Instead I'm walking around the classroom as my students complete the warm-up and addressing any problems I see.

- Because summative assessments hold a lot of weight in my system, I like to offer students the chance for test corrections as a means of regaining partial credit for errors at test time. I talk to my students about how test corrections are our version of a curve for a test. I remind them that the point is mastering the material and that test corrections give us another chance for doing that.

- I give students five emergency passes at the start of the semester that they can use for submitting late work; otherwise, I don't accept late work.

- I try entering no more than two or three things into the grade book in a given week. This saves me time doing data entry and reduces my opportunity for making errors entering grades. It also reduces complexity for students trying to improve their grades.

(Continued)

(Continued)

Overall, the most powerful thing we can do to help students who are obsessed with grades is to speak to the truth that our goal is mastery, not grades. I advise teachers to be as creative and passionate and consistent as they can be with little messages like this, which are typically spoken for the whole class to hear when the matter of grades comes up. At the same time, though, it's important to express compassion for students who are anxious about grades. This is a hard way to go through secondary school.

May our classrooms be rich in little nudges away from grade-mongering.

My Students Come From Homes Where Education Isn't Valued.

This one is easier to respond to. First, I've been teaching and parenting long enough to know that when educators make assumptions about a student's home life, there's a lot of ego blindness going on. I always tell colleagues, "The only home I can speak authoritatively on is the one I live in. And even then, there's a lot I don't know!"

Second, my students' homes are not contexts that I control, and therefore I do not spend time or energy fixated on what *may or may not* be valued in them. It is just not something I have found it profitable to attend to. But what I absolutely must attend to, with great vigor and earnestness, is the degree to which education is valued in *my* classroom. The person most responsible for the values of *that place* is *me*.

And that serves as a lovely segue into our next strategy: Micro-Sermons From an Apologist, Winsome and Sure.

Strategy 4: Micro-Sermons From an Apologist, Winsome and Sure

If our students are to see the Value of our disciplines, they need us to frequently communicate our vision of just how valuable our disciplines are. It is not primarily up to their families to communicate the Value of our subject areas, nor is it primarily up to the students themselves. First and foremost, it is our job as educators to communicate the Value of school. To do so, we must become the kinds of teachers who habitually and frequently make the case for schooling. We must become apologists, winsome and sure. The best path to becoming this kind of person is to give lots and lots of mini-sermons on the Value of what we do.

What to Do

- Once per class period or so, take around thirty seconds to tell your students why the work of learning that you ask them to do is valuable. You can do this at a pre-arranged time (e.g., the start or end of a lesson), or you can keep your eyes open for when the opportunity arises.

- As you're doing this, push yourself to cast a broad vision of how your discipline is useful. The Rainbow of Why can help with this. You want to be multichromatic—sometimes sermonize on the usefulness (utility) of your discipline, other times speak about its beauty.

- If you want to really push yourself, use the Rainbow of Why to contemplate the fullness of why what you teach is valuable. Brainstorm reasons on a blank sheet of paper or in a group of like-hearted colleagues.

- To keep yourself accountable to building the habit, use a simple checklist or daily routine to increase the frequency with which you explain to your students that the work you're all doing is deeply good.

Key Pointers

- This strategy is about becoming the *kind* of teacher from whom winsome and confident reasons for your discipline easily and frequently flow.

- Your sermonizing should be brief. It's more powerful to give lots of little micro-sermons over the course of a semester than it is to glaze your students' eyes with five-minute rants on how important school is.

How Strategy 4 Influences the Five Key Beliefs

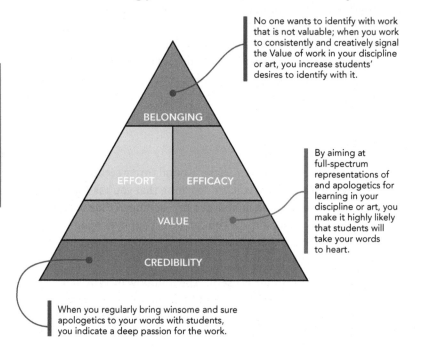

No one wants to identify with work that is not valuable; when you work to consistently and creatively signal the Value of work in your discipline or art, you increase students' desires to identify with it.

By aiming at full-spectrum representations of and apologetics for learning in your discipline or art, you make it highly likely that students will take your words to heart.

When you regularly bring winsome and sure apologetics to your words with students, you indicate a deep passion for the work.

Everything in this world means. It speaks. It sings. It's lovable.

ANDREW KERN

An Apologist . . .

Of the ten strategies featured in this book, I think it likely that this is the oddest one to grasp. And so, let me attempt to explain *what* I mean by "an apologist, winsome and sure." If I accomplish that, then I think the *why* will be fairly clear.

An apologist is someone who gives an account for something controversial. Our word *apologist* is rooted in Latin:

- *apo*—meaning "out from, away from, off of" (and so, an apologist is someone from whom a kind of thing comes)

- *logos*—meaning "reason" (and so, an apologist is someone deeply concerned with meaning and reason)

All together then, the word *apologist* in history has most often meant a person who brings forth from themselves well-reasoned words—specifically in defense of something controversial.

So Wait—Is the Value of an Education *That* Controversial?

In my estimation, there are two main avenues through which the average American will find school to be valuable:

1. If the things I'm learning in class today are things I can surely *use* in my future, then yes, school is valuable.

2. If the things I'm learning in class today are things that connect with my current interests and values, then yes, school is valuable.

In other words, a lesson must have utility or relevance. Otherwise, it's not all that worth learning. Because learning, in United States culture, just isn't all that meaningful.

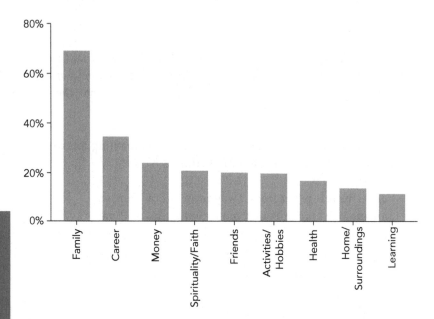

Value

Percentage of Americans Who Mention _____When Describing
What Provides Them With a Sense of Purpose.

*Source: "Where Americans Find Meaning in Life." Pew Research Center, Washington, D.C. (November
20, 2018) https://www.pewresearch.org/religion/2018/11/20/where-americans-find-meaning-in-life/.*

In my classroom experiences and those I hear about from all over, this
is deeply problematic from a motivational perspective, especially as
students advance into their secondary education. The older you get, the
more specialized the disciplines become. As specialization increases,
utility and relevance become decreasingly obvious. For example:

- It's fairly easy to argue that all students will use addition and
  subtraction someday; it's fairly hard to argue that students
  will use the Pythagorean Theorem.

- It's easy to argue that students will need to read throughout
  their lives; it's hard to argue that they'll *need* Shakespeare.

- It's easy to argue that students in the United States ought to
  know the significance of 1776; it's harder to argue that they
  need to grasp the reasons that 1776 both did and did not
  represent a revolutionary shift from prior history.

In other words, the only avenues for sustaining a strong and deep
Value belief as students age are those that get at the deeper and more

timeless goods of your discipline or art. It's less about the explicit moment at which you'll apply today's lesson and more about the timeless goodness and meaning and beauty that can be accessed through the pursuit of mastery of the disciplines or the arts. Beauty, goodness, meaning—these are the Value power strokes. What we're after in this strategy is becoming the kinds of folks from whom the case for the beauty and goodness and meaning of our class regularly flows.

. . . Who Is Winsome and Sure

When I first came up with this phrase to describe the type of apologists we need to be as teachers, the person I was envisioning was C. S. Lewis. Though most famous today for his Chronicles of Narnia, back in the mid-twentieth century Lewis was a well-renowned apologist. Having come to the Christian faith from a place of deep skepticism, he never relinquished his respect for folks who doubted the religion he had become so confident in.

His most famous work of apologetics, *Mere Christianity*, began as a set of talks on BBC radio during the dark times of World War II. Many were skeptical of Lewis's belief in a good and loving God. And Lewis, throughout his remarks, embodied a winsome and sure apologist.

He was *winsome*—a word whose root, *win*, comes from the Old English *wyn*, meaning "joy." Someone who is winsome speaks in a way that is engaging, attractive, appealing. Their language emanates joy. (And if you're wondering what this has to do with teaching, hang tight— we're about to see a math teacher put winsomeness on display.)

And he was *sure*—a word rooted in the Latin *securus*, meaning "free from care." Someone who is sure emanates confidence and certainty. They are not arrogant; they just calmly know that they stand on solid ground.

Let's Visit a Math Teacher.

Now this all sounds very theoretical, so let's bring our discussion down into a high school math classroom. Caroline Ong teaches in Texas, and what follows is a transcript from 2.5 minutes of her geometry class one day. To help you see what Caroline's apologetics are, I'll present Caroline's words with my analysis as footnotes.

"All right, we're going to look at two examples. You're gonna need to add these to your notes.[20] Let's say I have—let's see who we have— we have A.J. so, Point A over here, and we have Colton, so Point C[21] over here, and we are going to scale this up. They are ten miles apart. Okay. And then we have Mrs. Ong giving a vast lecture[22], so we're going to call this Point O. And, from A.J.'s point of view this angle is 45 degrees, and from Colton's point of view this angle is 35 degrees. I would like to find this side right here which I'm going to call *X*. How far am I from A.J.?"

"Okay, so we could actually act this out, and we could force Colton and A.J. to run in opposite directions until they are ten miles apart, and then I would adjust my position until the angles are appropriate, and then we could do a physical measurement of the distances.[23] Is that efficient? *No!* Okay, mathematics allows us to solve problems very efficiently—*we are so lazy!*—absolutely Kale! Mathematicians are lazy,[24] we want to find the most efficient way to solve a problem. Okay, that's one of the beauties[25] of mathematics is we're looking for the most efficient way to solve a problem.

"You guys! Okay, I'm going to get on my math is wonderful high horse for just a second.[26] *Life* is about finding the most efficient ways to solve

_____

[20]Caroline's making wise and strategic effort clear here: She's not leaving note-taking up to chance. This is Strategy 7: Woodenize All of It.

[21]Caroline is incorporating student names into her diagram of a triangle. This signals Belonging—your names are a part of the learning we do—and it signals the Value-conducive signals of whimsy and fun.

[22]She's teasing herself here; gently self-deprecating humor signals confidence and maturity. Both of these signals are boons to Credibility.

[23]She's modeling that there are many ways to solve a problem—including ways that are silly.

[24]This is clearly language that Caroline has used before—Kale spontaneously calls it out when she asks if her first solution method is efficient. But this language is also *novel*—students are unlikely to have heard from a teacher like Mrs. Ong before that mathematicians are lazy. Novelty helps build Value.

[25]Here she has introduced the *B* word—beauty—and it triggers her to her next move, the "math is wonderful high horse."

[26]"For just a second"—Caroline is gently urgent (Strategy 3).

problems.[27] You guys are going to go out, you're going to grow up one day, right?[28] Travis and I were talking about this morning[29]—you're not going to be a teenager forever! And you're going to go out and have some sort of life calling[30] and it's going to be about solving problems. Maybe you're solving building problems and you're an architect, okay? Maybe you're solving special education problems, and you're a teacher.[31]

"Life is about solving problems, and it's not *just* about solving problems.[32] It's solving problems in an efficient way, and it is solving problems in a way that other people can use in communicating your solution method to others. These are all things we do in math.[33] Math is beautiful.[34]

"Okay. So, we are not going to make a scale diagram of this, we're not going to make A.J. and Colton run and so forth, and so . . ."[35]

---

[27]She's connecting a key purpose of math—learning to solve problems—to her students' whole lives. This signals meaning and purpose.

[28]She's connecting to something all her high schoolers are concerned with—the fact that they are close to "going out" into the world. She's communicating this with confidence and passion—this is not a "Be scared of the real world, kids!" kind of message, but instead, "Oh how I delight in the thought of the world beyond school getting the pleasure of experiencing every one of you."

[29]She's referencing a conversation with a student—perhaps one that took place during an attempted MGC (Strategy 1). This indicates to all students that Mrs. Ong cares and talks with students.

[30]Meaning! Purpose!

[31]Caroline is drawing these example aspirations from the actual aspirations of some of the students in the room.

[32]Caroline is now presenting a multifaceted view of math—it's not just solving problems, it's solving them efficiently; it's not just solving them efficiently, it's being able to communicate clearly to others about those solutions.

[33]She's now connecting these three big and clear purposes for math to the things we do on a daily basis. The mundane is being infused with meaning.

[34]Short, profound. She makes an audacious statement. In the background at this moment, you can hear her students gently chuckling. They are delighted to be seeing a human being so overcome with goodness.

[35]And then she moves right along. She can sense the power in the room, *but she respects it enough not to draw it out*. The entire "high horse" monologue is only thirty seconds long. As a result, Caroline's room is one in which such moments can be *normal*—they don't mess up the flow of a lesson or require some immense planning on her part—and in their normality they send an other-worldly signal. Students can't help but be drawn along, further up and further in, to a deep and abiding belief in the Value of mathematics.

Caroline's Impact

Caroline's example—which you can watch using the QR code is the best explanation I can give for what Strategy 4 is all about. It's about becoming the kind of person from whom winsome, confident, and powerful arguments regularly flow.

Scan this QR code to watch a demonstration from Caroline Ong on mathematical sermonizing.

And now let's look at how to train ourselves to become this kind of person.

HOW TO GAIN PROFICIENCY WITH STRATEGY 4

Define and Communicate the Everest of the Course(s) You Teach.

A winsome and sure apologist possesses big picture clarity. To help with that, define the Everest for your course. To do this, answer questions like these:

- What is your course ultimately for? Your discipline or art?

- If you had to summarize your course in a sentence-length list of core outcomes, what would they be? What if you had to summarize it in a way that you could communicate in an off-the-cuff manner to students on a regular basis?

I call this the "Defining Everest" activity. Let me share a bunch of examples. (Steal at will!)

- In Caroline's geometry example, she says that math is about
    - learning to solve problems
    - in an efficient manner
    - that you can then communicate clearly to others.

- In AP computer science, Ms. Kate McDonnell in Denver, Colorado, says that
  - "my goal is to help my students be more prepared for the AP exams in the spring, especially reading tough free-response questions and being able to figure out how to answer them."
- In agricultural science, Mr. Brent Willett from Cedar Springs, Michigan, says his class helps students
  - "develop leadership, life skills, and career success through hands-on experiences, labs, and trips that students would otherwise not experience at home."
- In music and band, Mr. John Hawk from Arkansas believes that
  - "through teaching music and band I can help my students become good citizens. *Good* meaning kind, responsible, problem solvers and hard workers."
- In Spanish, Ms. Amy Holmes from Michigan, says,
  - "My class is for making an insane amount of errors while trying to make meaning in order to love and understand more people."
- In Spanish, Ms. Tanya Ramm from Michigan, says that
  - "after taking any class in our world language department, our students will be better communicators in the target language and open up their eyes and hearts to appreciate other cultures."
- In French, Ms. Erica Kencke in Oregon envisions that
  - "every single one of my students will experience thinking in French at some level, recognize that that is what they are doing, and be encouraged by that to learn more."
- In my English language arts classes, I say that we are all about becoming
  - better thinkers,
  - better readers,
  - better writers,
  - better speakers and listeners, and
  - better people.

Value

- In phys ed, an anonymous teacher believes that
  - physical education teaches us to enjoy and care for our physical selves.
- In physical science, Mr. Tyler Kee, a teacher of ninth graders in Arkansas, believes that students will grow
  - more capable of critical thinking in new situations,
  - more knowledgeable about the world they live in, and
  - more imaginative about life in general.
- In his science classes, Mr. Steve Vree in Michigan envisions that students will
  - proficiently learn, explain, and apply science disciplinary core ideas (DCIs) while learning, practicing, and demonstrating science and engineering practices (SEPs) and cross-cutting concepts (CCCs).
- In chemistry, Mr. Tyler Weatherwax in Michigan says that
  - "students learn to ask questions and make observations that lead to developing ideas or understandings that might help us solve problems or make predictions."
- In her visual arts classes, Ms. Jen Swift in Cedar Springs, Michigan, hopes that her students
  - experience the joy and benefits of experimenting while creating art and observe that there are multiple perspectives and ways to achieve an outcome.

Once you've got a draft of your Everest, drop everything and communicate it. Run it by your colleagues and especially your students. Hang it up on your wall.

Go Full Jackson Pollock With the Rainbow of Why.

Here we return to the Rainbow of Why, but instead of using it to understand how hearts arrive at Value, we'll use it as a springboard for creativity, fun, color, and spontaneity.

To help you see what I mean, let's consider the work of one of the twentieth century's most influential painters, Jackson Pollock, known for his splattery, streaky, "action painting" method.[36]

Here's how Pollock approached his painting, and here's how I love to see teachers approach their micro-sermons:

- He was *bold.*
- He was *countercultural*—he created *Number 1* in 1949, about the same time as cookie-cutter communities like Levittown were becoming popular.
- He was *energetic.*
- He had this *"made-on-the-fly" feel* to his style.

the **RAINBOW** of **WHY**

- utility
- relevance
- social status
- autonomy
- justice, prosocial
- novelty
- enjoyment, pleasure
- meaning, purpose
- beauty

pexels.com/Steve Johnson

These descriptors, to me, have a lot in common with how we can become apologists, winsome and sure and *have a great time doing it.*

---

[36]For a classic example, you can see Pollock's *Number 1* (1949) at https://davestu artjr.com/pollock.

The Rainbow of Why is a painter's palette for a reason: I want you to view Value cultivation as a creative work, an exploratory work, a

COLOR ON THE RAINBOW OF WHY	QUESTION(S) TO GET YOU MICRO-SERMONIZING (USE THESE AS JUMPING-OFF POINTS FOR YOUR MICRO-SERMONS)
Utility	• How is what you teach useful? • How does what you teach allow students to do what they previously would not have been able to do? • When will students use what you teach?
Relevance	• How does what you teach connect specifically to the real-world interests or values of at least one of your students? • What's an interest you know at least some of your students have? How does that link up with today's lesson?
Social Status	• How could what your students are learning about in your class make them cooler? • How could what they're learning redefine "cool"? • How could what they are learning help them relate to others in new and more profound ways?
Autonomy	• How does what you teach give students power either now or later in life? • How is what you teach powerful?
Justice, Prosocial	• How can the work you do in your discipline or art make the world a better, fairer, more just place? • How can mastery of your discipline or art make it easier to help others?
Novelty	• What do most folks not realize about what you teach that if they *did* realize would give them a whole different view about why your discipline or art is good?
Enjoyment, Pleasure	• What's fun about what you teach? • What enjoyment or pleasure do you get from your discipline?
Meaning, Purpose	• How does what your students are learning connect with what it means to be a human being? • How does what they're learning tap into their deepest desires for their lives—desires to make a difference, to be independent, to be understood?
Beauty	• What is beautiful about what you teach? • Why is what you teach beautiful?

beautiful work. It's not a have-to, it's a *get-to*. It's not just a job, it's a *joy*. I want you to paint with these colors like Jackson Pollock. Be bold, be countercultural, be energetic, be okay with "on-the-fly" action painting.

Let's look at each color on the Rainbow of Why and envision what that might look like.

Here are examples of answers to some of these questions from real teachers of real students:

- Rear Admiral Grace Hopper was a decorated math professor for the U.S. Navy. When her students complained about being graded for writing in her math classes, she would tell them that there was "no use trying to learn math unless [you] can communicate with other people" (Heath & Starr, 2022, p. 36)

- Brian Busen is a personal finance teacher in Cedar Springs, Michigan. On the first day of class, he tells his students, "Welcome to personal finance. My name is Mr. Busen and let me start off by letting you know up front that, aside from a religious class or teachings, this class will be the most impactful and important class from a financial and relational perspective than any class you will ever take in your lifetime." Notice his surety!

- When Erica Beaton was in the classroom as an ELA teacher, she would have her students create a research-informed argument on a justice-related current issue. Beaton would often remind her students that the papers they were writing were going to be read by people outside of her room and that there was a real chance that a well-written paper could result in changing someone's mind and thereby making a real change in the world.

- I will sometimes remark to my students how cool it is to know things. I tell them this class is not about becoming a slightly awkward and bespectacled middle-aged man who knows a bunch about literature and world history. Instead I say, "No! It's about being a teenager just like you who knows a bunch about literature and world history. How cool are you as you keep growing your knowledge in these areas! It is cool to know things!"

- Caroline Ong's example (from several pages ago) does a good job connecting the work of mathematics with some of the future careers her students would like to have. She also taps into meaning and purpose when she references that her students are growing up.

- An agricultural science teacher in Linden, California, tells her culinary students that "we are the fork to the community's farm."

Practice Your Apologetics When You Talk With Your Colleagues, When You Walk With Yourself, and When You Brush Your Teeth.

If we're to become teachers like Caroline Ong—folks from whom flow a constant stream of instinctive and imaginative and winsome apologetics—we've got to practice, practice, practice, practice.

One obvious time to do this, of course, is during our lessons when we're with students. Indeed, this is so important that it gets its own treatment in the next section. Some less obvious ideas for practicing, however, are the following:

- As you're brushing your teeth in the morning before school, imagine a student walking up to you and saying, "Dear teacher, I need help! I don't see how what we're learning in class has anything good it can give me. I'd like to find Value in it, but alas—I cannot." Think of your response while you're brushing, and then once you've finished your hygiene, stare into your eyes in the mirror and give the best response you can muster. It's important here to start talking right away—sometimes the mouth guides the mind.

- I think all teachers benefit from a ten-minute walk each workday. I like to do this via what I call "five-out-five-in": At the start of my prep, I set a timer for five minutes and walk away from my classroom and directly toward as much nature or solitude as I can find. I keep walking until the five minute timer goes off, and then I turn around and walk back. The whole exercise only lasts ten minutes, but when I neglect to do it, I notice a decrease in the health of my inner world. On such walks, I sometimes imagine a particular student who is struggling with Value, and—when I've walked far enough from my school that folks won't think me completely crazy—I begin speaking aloud my response to this student's desire for the work of learning in my room to have actual, substantial, and lasting Value.

- Even the most introverted among us have regular conversations with colleagues. Quite infrequent, though, are the times in which these conversations transcend the mundane ("So-and-so said such-and-such and I did this-and-that"). Next time, try infusing some apologetics into your discourse.

Here's what can come from practicing in these three ways every day that you work:

- First, you get 180 days of thrice-a-day practice (teeth brushing, walk-and-talk, collegial conversation), which amounts to over five hundred repetitions at your apologetics. I dare you to emerge from such a regimen unchanged.
- Second, you'll develop a reputation as someone who is crazy about what you do; this will aid your Credibility in ways you'll never quantify but will surely sense with time.

And, of course, all the while you'll be getting even *more* practice during your classes with students. Let's turn to that now.

Incorporate Your Apologetics Into Every Single Lesson *as Simply as You Can.*

Did you notice that I emphasized that last part? Good. That's really important. There are several places in which I've known teachers to habitually insert apologetics into their lessons: the start-of-class lesson rationale, the thirty-second high horse, the spontaneous micro-nerdout, and the end-of-class sermon. Let's treat each of these places in turn.

Where to Fit Apologetics Into a Basic Lesson Structure

lesson rationale	**Warm-up**	• students working independently • teacher attempting an MGC • teacher completing admin tasks
	Lesson intro/ go over warm-up	• teacher or students provide lesson rationale • students share warm-up work • teacher gives whole-class feedback
30-second high horse or micro-nerdout	**Lesson chunk 1**	• students read or listen to a knowledge-rich text • teacher provides direct instruction and guided practice • teacher models how to put forth wise effort in learning
	Lesson chunk 2	• students read or listen to a knowledge-rich text • teacher provides direct instruction and guided practice • teacher models how to put forth wise effort in learning
	Lesson chunk 3	• students read or listen to a knowledge-rich text • teacher provides direct instruction and guided practice • teacher models how to put forth wise effort in learning
mini-sermon	**Tie it all together**	• teacher leads reflective application of today's lesson • students make connections
	Closing	• teacher gives mini-sermon on value of lesson students engage in engaging retrieval practice (e.g., Quizlet, Kahoot, Gimkit, Blooket)

Value

The start-of-class lesson rationale is a fine place for a micro-sermon. Right after the warm-up, as you're introducing the lesson objective, answer the thought-bubble question mark that's floating over some of your students' heads: Why this lesson? Why today? *Why's it matter?*

The thirty-second high horse is one we've already seen. It's when you spontaneously launch into a mini-monologue about why what we're learning is good.

The spontaneous micro-nerdout is when you see a student applying something they've learned and you briefly make a big deal out of it. Here's an example that junior high ELA colleague Angie Morley in Utah related to me:

> At the beginning of the year (Term 1), I teach students the three uses of a dash (pause, substitution, parentheses) through the short story "Thank You Ma'am" by Langston Hughes. Students start with teacher examples, then create group-generated examples, and finally individually written examples of each type of dash. (Incidentally, the dash is part of the English 8 conventions standards.)
>
> During Term 2-4 writing, I consistently highlight students' use of each type of dash in their writing. Often, we review student samples of writing for class editing of mechanics and/or analysis of organizational and idea elements. None of these review sessions are focused specifically on using a dash in writing. Still, *there's a positive momentum that builds around dash use when I highlight students who are doing it well.* In Term 2 a few brave souls began incorporating a dash element in their writing. As I spotlighted these efforts, e.g., "Jane, that's an impressive use of a substitution dash—well done," more and more students began using a dash in their writing. Now, instead of a few brave souls, I have a significant number of students who are increasing their sentence sophistication through dash use. This all began in a Term 2 collaborative writing session where one student's use of the dash led to several others making a brave attempt during the same period.

Note that this kind of nerdout can be done in matters unrelated to your discipline or art, too.

- If you're showing a brief YouTube clip as part of today's lesson and the videographer or presenter does something smart or admirable or clever or beautiful, pause the video and nerd out about it for a second. For example, you might say, "Oh my goodness, students, did you see what she did there? That was amazing. I loved that."

- If you're reading something with your students and a feature of the text stands out, explain why it stands out. What's remarkable about it?

Value is like the universe—there's no scarcity if you just zoom out (or in) far enough.

Ask Your Colleagues What Wonders They See in What They Teach.

Winsome and sure apologists are contagious! So ask your colleagues questions like these once in a while:

- What makes what you teach special?
- What's one of your favorite things about your discipline or art?
- What's one of the most exciting things about your discipline or art right now?

COMMON TEACHER HANG-UPS

If a Student Can't Find Utility or Relevance to Their Life in What We're Teaching, Then What We're Teaching Doesn't Matter.

My only answer to this is the Rainbow of Why. There are so many more pathways to Value than utility and relevance. To drive this home, I sometimes answer the student asking "When will we ever use this?" like this, with a big grin on my face: "Maybe never. I'm not sure. But it's still so, so, so, so good. Just wait. You'll see." The grin is winsome. The statement is sure. I think we'd see a radical positive movement of the Value belief in our schools if we'd do more winsome and sure apologetics.

By the Time Students Are in Secondary School, Isn't It Too Late to Start Convincing Them That Their Education Is Valuable?

It's true: The very best time to start inundating students with frequent, authentic, and passionate micro-sermons about the Value of learning is the day that they start school as little ones and every day thereafter. The more of these kinds of signals you receive as a human being, the more likely you are to interpret them as the norm. If you're flooded with this stuff consistently from the time that you're young, you are super likely to both experience and embody a culture in which learning is deeply and beautifully and meaningfully good.

But the second best time to begin such efforts—and the only time over which you and I can exert any control—is today. For the sake of our future students, we can spread the good word that a credible teacher's thirty-second micro-sermon is never wasted time—even for the youngest of learners. But for the sake of our current students, today is the best day to get started.

Strategy 5: A Feast of Knowledge
(Or: Teach Stuff, Lots)

Though we live in a time where most things can be Googled, when it comes to student motivation the distance between knowledge and a search query is a gaping canyon. The Internet, rightly conceived, is a boon to learning, not a replacement for it. We want our students to have knowledge constellations all throughout their minds. Strategy 5, then, is about making the Value belief possible by giving our students a chance to know lots of things. After all, it's pretty hard to value something you know nothing about. Therefore, a strong path to the Value belief is a knowledge-rich curriculum and classroom.

What to Do

- Whatever you teach, teach all that you know about it. You want your class to feel like a tour through the cosmos of your discipline. Whether it's literature or science or economics or health, show your students through your knowledge-rich lessons, curricula, and asides that there is great glory in the quest of learning.

- While you're the main tour guide on this trip through your disciplinary cosmos, you need not be the only one. As you come across interesting articles, videos, films, or books, ask yourself, *How could I give my students a taste of this? How might I expose them to just a bit more knowledge without totally dismantling my curriculum?*

- Establish and teach students to memorize "sets of knowns."[37] These are lists of core facts that through your course will become dense with meaning.

- When in doubt, bias yourself toward an expansive knowledge feast. You need not stick to curriculum with 100 percent of the minutes you are given to teach.

------

[37]This is a term from Tammy Elser, one of Montana's great literacy minds.

Key Pointer

- You want to create a classroom where learning things is good because learning things is good. As it turns out, it's hard to create a room like that when all students ever get to learn are content-agnostic skills. So, *teach stuff!*

How Strategy 5 Influences the Five Key Beliefs

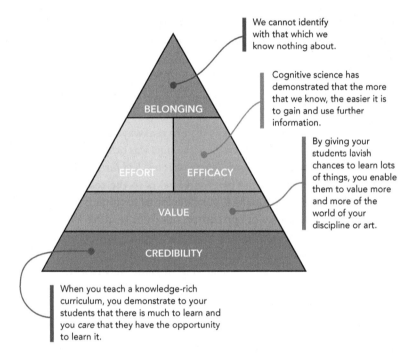

We cannot identify with that which we know nothing about.

Cognitive science has demonstrated that the more that we know, the easier it is to gain and use further information.

By giving your students lavish chances to learn lots of things, you enable them to value more and more of the world of your discipline or art.

When you teach a knowledge-rich curriculum, you demonstrate to your students that there is much to learn and you *care* that they have the opportunity to learn it.

I've come to think that one main reason our students are bored is because we've taught them so little. I can remember the moment in my classroom when this began to haunt me. Several years ago I gave my ninth-grade students a scenario to write about as their warm-up:

> Ninth graders around the United States are having a hard time caring about school. To some, it's so boring or pointless that they consider dropping out—even in ninth grade. Imagine you are writing an article to these ninth graders

and that your goal is to convince them to finish—and even enjoy—their K-12 education. What would you say in your letter?[38]

After the writing I had students pair up and share what they wrote. Then I took volunteers to share with the whole class. And Jayke's response, especially, left a mark on me.

Basically, Jayke argued that students should apply themselves to their studies because doing so would help them learn things, and learning things—"putting knowledge in your head," as Jayke put it—makes it possible *to think thoughts that you otherwise couldn't think.*

I was blown away. Jayke, a fourteen-year-old barely two weeks into his high school career, had intuited that there was such a thing as a life of the mind, that this life was in very real ways inseparable from all the rest of life, and that *this life of the mind was richer or poorer for the ideas and concepts and fact constellations that one had furnished it with.* In other words, Jayke beat me by twenty years to the realization that knowledge doesn't just make it possible for us to think critically and argue well and learn faster and comprehend our reading. What Jayke figured out is that *knowledge is what we think with*; to put it another way, *we think from and with what we know,* and due to the centrality of our thoughts to our lives, *we live from what we know.* In this way, *knowing things actually shapes who we are.* Knowledge, to bring it back to Dallas Willard's language, shapes our *souls.*

So, what happens when we spend years of lesson time focused on test-aligned, knowledge-lite skills? We end up perseverating opportunity gaps and impoverishing our students' ability to think, to learn, to engage, and to *be* as they grow older in our K-12 systems.

---

[38]This is a classic example of a "student as expert" prompt, which we explore further in Strategy 10 on page 230. Basically, placing students in the position of expert, where they tell someone else why they ought to care about _____, makes it more likely that their beliefs about a topic will shift.

The less I know about a subject, the more boring that subject is—that was Jayke's claim. And I think he saw it in the hallways in the ways his peers treated one another and also in our ever-truncating political discourse.

Knowing things makes *life*—including the part of life we spend in school—more exciting and interesting and fulfilling and grand. This was Jayke's argument. And, in my view, Jayke was irrefutably right.

It's impossible to value things that you know nothing about. Let me give you two examples: one from children I've never met and one from my younger days as a college undergraduate.

In *The Knowledge Gap*, journalist Natalie Wexler (2019) describes Canaan Elementary, a school with a knowledge-rich curriculum.[39] At first teachers were hesitant to teach students lots of things—after all, in the age of Google, why teach facts? Interestingly, according to Wexler, "It was recess that really changed teachers' minds."

Wexler goes on to say that

> recess tended to be a free-form affair, with no regard to rules even during games like soccer. But then the teachers noticed that their second-graders were playing Greek gods and goddesses—with rules.

> "So they are forming themselves in clusters," [one of the teachers] says, "telling this little girl, 'Well you can't be our Athena,' but they need an Athena, 'but if you want to be Artemis then we're good to go, because we don't have one yet.'"

> The second-graders also used a large map of the United States in the playground to recap the tall tales and legends they were learning. A kid would stand inside the outline of, say, Minnesota, and tell the story of Paul Bunyon and his blue ox. The same thing happened with the kindergarteners:

---

[39] In other words, with a curriculum that teaches students lots of things about lots of things.

during their unit on rocks, they devoted recess to that subject for almost two weeks, ignoring the swings.

"All they wanted to do was dig around," says [the teacher], "because they were rock-hounding all day every day, trying to talk to each other about the things they found and things they didn't, about the things they were encountering" (p. 207).

That's motivation in a nutshell: when learning becomes play.

In my own life, knowledge enabled me to appreciate cultural diversity in a way that I previously was incapable of. I grew up in the racially homogenous rural town of Middleville, Michigan. Nearly all of my friends and classmates were white, and nearly all of us grew up in the same rural locale. This was the case all the way through my K-12 education.

But then for my undergrad, I moved across the state to Ann Arbor to study at the University of Michigan. In my freshman dormitory hallway, my neighbors represented dozens of combinations of racial, ethnic, religious, and national backgrounds. My naïveté—the result of a dearth of knowledge and experience—led to conversations reminiscent of Acho's (2020) *Uncomfortable Conversations With a Black Man*.

But the more I *learned* about the experiences of folks different from me, the more *engaged* I became. Within a couple of years, I was an eager and grateful tutor for the Telluride Association's Sophomore Seminar—a program that invited high school sophomores from around the United States to come to Ann Arbor for a six-week summer intensive focused on African American studies. I still recall with fondness the late-night discussions I was blessed to have with BIPOC students from across the United States— conversations sprinkled with diverse personal experiences and allusions to the works of intellectuals like Malcolm X, James Baldwin, Toni Morrison, Maya Angelou, and Robert Hayden.

My point with all of this is to demonstrate anecdotally a truth meted out by the cognitive science research: It's impossible to value something that you know nothing about, but the more you learn the more chance you have of coming to value a subject *without even trying to.* Value, curiosity, interest—these things tend to align with domains we have a *grid* for, things that we *know* something about.

In short: *knowledge begets motivation.*

- It turns learning into play.
- It opens our minds to new learning, experiences, and people.
- It enables critical thinking and reading comprehension.[40]

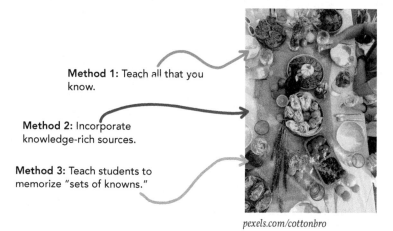

Method 1: Teach all that you know.

Method 2: Incorporate knowledge-rich sources.

Method 3: Teach students to memorize "sets of knowns."

pexels.com/cottonbro

Three Easy (and Fun) Angles to Hosting a Feast of Knowledge in Your Classroom

Think of Strategy 5 as a giant feast. All of your favorite foods are there: all the apps, all the main courses, all the desserts, all the drinks. This is the endgame of what we're doing here for our students—we're inviting them in to taste and see that our disciplines and arts are good,

---

[40]For an in-depth treatment of this, see Chapter 3 of *These 6 Things: How to Focus Your Teaching on What Matters Most* (Stuart, 2018).

that there are smells and sensations here that outside of what we're teaching they can never know.

With this picture of a feast-laden table in mind, let's now consider paths to the table that we can walk along with our students. As we practice these, let's remember what we're preparing our students for. It's not a test. It's not something they'll use someday to earn more money. Nope. It's a *feast*.

Method 1: Teach All That You Know.

First, teach all that you know! A quick caveat, however. Let me ask you a question: Have you ever seen a teacher come into your school, last name followed by all sorts of degree letters but with *zero sense* of how to engage, motivate, or manage students in a real classroom? I have seen my fair share.

The thing with teaching all that you know is that you have to be mindful that you're doing this with *human beings*. Very few of your students want to *watch you* eat a feast. But *all* of your students want to *experience* a feast.

Here are some examples of teaching all that you know:

- In a health course, tell students about a study that you came across recently that relates to one of the units they've learned this year or will learn before the course ends.

- In a drawing course, show a student a piece you created recently, or do a series of warm-ups in which you share with them ten of your favorite paintings of all time.

- In a physical education course, begin class one day by showing students a brief YouTube video of a person completing a massive squat in the weight room. Point out for students how this person is practicing the principles that they are practicing in your class.

- In an ELA course, share your personal pursuits as a writer or a reader.

Value

- In a calculus course, respond to a student question by briefly explaining how the question points to content that's outside the scope of Calculus I but was a big focus in the Calculus III course you took in college.

- In a government course, share the presidential campaign you volunteered for while in college.

- In a mathematics course, implement a "Future Friday" segment in which you share with students a brief blurb or video regarding a career field that regularly uses math.[41]

Blessedly, these knowledge-rich asides, as brief as they are, can fit just about anywhere in the basic, effective lesson anatomy that I laid out on page 86. You can

- include them in your warm-ups,
- include them as you introduce your lesson,
- include them in your main learning chunks, and/or
- include them in your lesson closings.

[41]Props to the math team in Hillsboro, Wisconsin, for this idea!

VALUE: **Strategy 5: A Feast of Knowledge** | 149

Where to Fit Knowledge-Rich Asides Into a Basic, Effective Lesson Structure

Value	**Warm-up**	• students working independently • teacher attempting an MGC • teacher completing admin tasks
wherever and whenever they make sense to you!	**Lesson intro/ go over warm-up**	• teacher or students provide lesson rationale • students share warm-up work • teacher gives whole-class feedback
	Lesson chunk 1	• students read or listen to a knowledge-rich text • teacher provides direct instruction and guided practice • teacher models how to put forth wise effort in learning
	Lesson chunk 2	• students read or listen to a knowledge-rich text • teacher provides direct instruction and guided practice • teacher models how to put forth wise effort in learning
	Lesson chunk 3	• students read or listen to a knowledge-rich text • teacher provides direct instruction and guided practice • teacher models how to put forth wise effort in learning
	Tie it all together	• teacher leads reflective application of today's lesson • students make connections
	Closing	• teacher gives mini-sermon on value of lesson students engage in engaging retrieval practice (e.g., Quizlet, Kahoot, Gimkit, Blooket)

Method 2: Incorporate Knowledge-Rich Sources.

The great news about the feast of knowledge is that you need not be the only chef. For example, YouTube has matured to the point where every discipline and art has numerous high-quality channels dedicated to teaching folks from beginner to advanced. The important thing with YouTube viewing is that you use videos interactively. This means that

- students are taking notes, often guided by you, on the material they learn and
- you are pausing the video periodically to model note-taking or to point out something the video's author has said or modeled that links with what you'd like students to take away from the video.

These points are so important—otherwise, as soon as the lights dim and the teacher clicks the red play icon, students will tend to zone out into *content consumption mode* rather than *knowledge construction mode*.

The world of blogs has matured as well during the past ten years. Quality, engaging articles on self-improvement and self-exploration in about any subject are available, such as the following:

- Benny the Irish Polyglot (fluentinthreemonths.com) is a favorite of foreign language teachers, as his articles cover language acquisition in various languages and they tend to be short and focused.
- Bulletproof Musician (bulletproofmusician.com) is a favorite stop for music teachers looking for a periodic article for students on the art and science of practice.

Method 3: Teach Students to Memorize Sets of Knowns.

The term *sets of knowns* comes from one of the most brilliant literacy thinkers I've ever met: our colleague Tammy Elser, who works as a professor and consultant in western Montana. Tammy has taught teachers for decades on Montana's 1999 Indian Education for All (IEFA) Act, which requires state educators to incorporate Native American education across the curricula. Tammy likes to tell the story of one of the first things she does with teachers during an IEFA workshop: She asks them to fill out a blank map of Montana's eight tribal nations, twelve tribes, and seven reservations.

This is an eye-opening experience for teachers, as many cannot complete the map to even 50 percent accuracy. Tammy then asks them to consider if it's likely they'll provide a quality Native American education for all if they cannot locate and name Montana's main groups of indigenous peoples.

This can also be the case for our students. How do we expect them to create complex thoughts, experience intellectual breakthroughs, or even gain basic comprehension of course concepts if we've not gifted them with a chance to commit foundational knowledge to memory? What I recommend for remedying this is to first identify foundational sets of knowns for your subject area, then guide your students to memorize these over time.

Here are some examples of sets of knowns by content area:

- For writing, rules for comma usage in Doug Stark's *Mechanics Instruction That Sticks*
- For world history, dates of significant events or geographic locations important to a given time period
- For U.S. history, questions from the U.S. citizenship test, or dates and locations significant to U.S. history
- For a course in computer applications, keyboard shortcuts that make working on a computer more efficient

My old boss Anne Kostus used to call these kinds of things our "Jay Leno lists" as a reference to those old bits where Jay Leno would walk the streets of New York City asking random passersby questions about basic disciplinary knowledge.

So how do I teach my students to memorize sets of knowns? In my history classes, I want my students to memorize a handful of what I call "must-know dates." My ninth-grade AP world history students memorize about 120 of them; my ninth-grade general world history students learn about 70.

Here's a sampling from our unit on Revolutions of the Long Nineteenth Century:

- 1776—American Declaration of Independence + Adam Smith writes *Wealth of Nations*
- 1791—Olympe de Gouge's Declaration of the Rights of Women
- 1804—Haitian Revolution
- 1815—Congress of Vienna (Europe's "balance of power" established)
- 1848—Marx and Engles publish *The Communist Manifesto*
- 1839—1st Opium War in China (sign of declining Qing dominance)
- 1861—End of serfdom in Russia
- 1863—Emancipation Proclamation in USA

Near the start of the school year, before I give my students their first list like this, I sometimes have them write a one-hundred-word quick warm-up on the following prompts: Are you the kind of person who can memorize a list of dates? How do you know? What kinds of things in your life do you memorize, and how do you do that?

We do some Pair-Share after kids have written for five minutes, and then I say, "Okay, get out a few sheets of blank scrap paper." I then lead them in the following steps:

- Step One: "Write down the list on the projector screen in its entirety." (I limit this initial list to five dates/events.) "In a minute, I'm going to have you write these from memory." (Student scoffing ensues.)
- Step Two: "Cover up your list, and now write that list of dates from memory." (I black out the projector at this point.) "Write down *every fragment* that you can remember—every bit of numbers, every bit of event description. It's okay to be wrong—get as much down as you can." (I give one to two minutes here, and I'm circulating the room to monitor how they're doing.)

- Step Three: "Get out your initial list, the one we copied from the projector screen. Let's call this List 1. I want you to use List 1 to correct List 2. Give yourself a score out of ten—one point for every correct date, and one point for every correct event description. And then I want you to make List 2 perfect, just like List 1. Cross things out, erase, use arrows, but make List 2 perfect. That's important."

- Step Four: "Cover up Lists 1 and 2 and, once again, write the list from memory." (I again black out the screen.) "This will be List 3."

- Step Five: "Okay. Get out Lists 1 and 2 and use them to correct List 3. Again, give yourself a score, and again, make List 3 perfect, like Lists 1 and 2. How many people improved their score from List 2 to List 3?" (At this point, almost all hands go up.)

- Step Six: "Okay, you get the idea. I want you to do it one more time, even if you just got a perfect score with List 3. Cover up Lists 1-3, and create a fourth and final list."

- Step Seven: "Correct, score, and make List 4 perfect."

- Step Eight: "Back in the warm-ups section of your notebooks, answer these questions afresh in writing: Are you the kind of person who can memorize dates? What do you do to memorize information like this? How long does it take? How hard is it?"

I typically end this with a chance for kids to share what they learned from the experience, and as they do this I punctuate their remarks with my own comments and arguments on why memorizing dates— and memorization in general—matters.

So, what's going on in this simple, fifteen-minute activity?

First of all, this date memorization stuff is one pillar of the year-long feast of knowledge we're seeking to enjoy together. I want to help all my students learn as much as they can while they're with me. Knowledge is inextricable from all the other things I want for them. It doesn't matter that there's Google—I want it in their *brains*, and I want to show them that there's a lot of unadvertised joy in this old-fashioned idea of building knowledge. This is why knowledge is one of the six things I address in *These Six Things: How to Focus Your Teaching on the Work That Matters Most.*

Also, I'm adding bricks to the Five Key Beliefs I want all my kids to hold while they're in my room.

- Credibility: The kids now know that I'm a teacher who can help them do things they didn't think they could do, and I can do it fairly quickly. I do *more* than say, "Work harder, punk." I teach them.

- Value: I'm planting seeds for why memorization matters. My arguments for the Value of memorization are one track toward helping them value this work.

- Effort: I'm showing the kids that rightly applied Effort can quickly make them more knowledgeable about history.

- Efficacy: By limiting the list to five dates and explicitly guiding them in the memorization process, I'm proving that success is possible.

- Belonging: Especially with the opening and closing writing exercises, I'm helping my kids to see themselves as the kinds of people who can do the work I'll ask them to do.

Just don't forget this:

Memorizing sets of knowns is really only effective (and is so much easier) when the knowledge is meaningful. If your sets of knowns aren't marinated in meaningful practice, then they won't stick. If I just have the kids memorize dates during one lesson and then never revisit them in subsequent lessons, readings, writings, or discussions, the dates won't stick and they won't matter.

Knowledge-building must be *meaningful*—toward this we must labor *constantly.*

COMMON TEACHER HANG-UPS

My Students Are at a Basic Level. Won't Teaching Them More Knowledge Overwhelm Them?

When we first got a piano (through one of those "free if you pick it up" listings on Craigslist), I knew nothing about it except that the keys made sound. That was it. I was at a basic level, through and through. No amount of motivation could remedy my limitation. I needed knowledge.

Everything changed once I learned how to play a few simple chords: C, G, D, and E minor. Then I was able to put the chords together and play some songs that I actually enjoyed. A little knowledge made it possible to move from basic to *delighted*. Nowadays, my pulse quickens when I see a piano. I think, *I can do some stuff on that thing, some stuff that's pretty.* Knowledge changed it all. Knowledge unlocks doors for learners at all levels.

If I Teach My Students All These Extra Things, Doesn't That Mean I Need to Assess and Grade Them on Their Mastery of the Additional Material?

No. For sure not. *Feasts aren't assessed.* What you're doing here is creating a sense in your room that the discipline or art we're studying is so, so, so, so, so much bigger than any test or assessment or grade.

When my students ask, "Will this be graded?" at the start of each school year, I delight in saying, "Probably not! It's so much bigger and better than that. The more we learn, the easier and better it will all become. So learn!"

Strategy 6: Valued Within

"Valued Within" is a set of learning activities designed to guide students to their own reasons for valuing school. These activities help students habituate the life-critical task of valuing something for their own reasons rather than those of others.

In our hyperindividualistic society, this student-generated approach to Value likely sounds superior to Strategy 4's teacher-generated one. In my practice and research, however, I have seen that we need schools in which both student- *and* teacher-generated approaches to Value are as ubiquitous as oxygen. Students need practice in *generating* Value for the work of learning within themselves *and* they need to have adults *modeling* this Value for them, all day long. By using this strategy, we grow more capable of helping students do the Value work themselves.

What to Do

Periodically guide your students to contemplate Value via some or all of the following activities:

- Hulleman's utility-value intervention (discussed on pages 160–163)
- simple *why* conversations (discussed on pages 163–165)
- finding the discipline or art you're teaching them in the world (discussed on page 165)

How Strategy 6 Influences the Five Key Beliefs

Because you've made space for student-generated value realizations, they're gaining a knack for the educational super-habit of figuring out why learning matters to *them*.

Interventional research shows that "valued within" methods correlate strongly to long-lasting positive effects on the degree to which students come to value a given art or discipline.

Students sense that you care when they are given opportunities to find connections between what they value and what they are learning in your class.

WHY THIS STRATEGY

There are two primary avenues a teacher should take in cultivating the Value belief in the hearts of students: teacher-generated signal-sending—we looked at this in Strategy 4—and student-generated Value-identification—we'll look at this now.

Two Approaches to Value
Cultivation in the Classroom

pexels.com/Steve Johnson

**teacher-generated
signal-sending**

+ generating is more
in your control
− likelihood of an
attempt succeeding
long term is lower

(you want to use both)

**student-generated
idenification**

− generating is less
in your control
+ likelihood of an
attempt succeeding
long term is higher

Value

It's important to realize that there are strengths and weaknesses to both the teacher and student-generated approaches to Value cultivation.

Teacher-generated approaches are entirely within our control—this is their main strength. They are also amplified by our Crediblity, so when we work hard to help students believe that we're good at our jobs, we'll also end up increasing the likelihood that our passion for our subjects will rub off onto them. The main weakness of teacher-generated approaches is that their effects can diminish over time. If our students are solely relying on us to figure out why our discipline matters, it makes sense that they may struggle with Value in the future with a teacher who is less explicit or passionate about the Value of this kind of work.

Student-generated approaches, on the other hand, do not have this weakness. If we can guide our students to practice determining the Value of our discipline themselves, we increase the chances that they'll value the discipline in the future *regardless* of how passionate or explicit about that Value their future teachers are. The trouble, of course, is that guiding students to practice Value cultivation within themselves is a much more complex endeavor than playing around with the language of a winsome and sure apologist that we looked at in Strategy 4.

In short, the optimal path to Value cultivation in a classroom and a school is to use both the teacher- and the student-generated approaches. Thankfully, a utility-value intervention from the research provides us with a strong hint at what such approaches can look like. We'll begin our exploration of how to gain proficiency with Strategy 6 by looking at this kind of intervention and its applications to secondary classrooms.

HOW TO GAIN PROFICIENCY WITH STRATEGY 6

Try a Monthly or Quarterly Utility-Value Intervention.

In a paper published in 2016, University of Wisconsin researcher Harackiewicz et al. shared the results of a utility-value intervention given to an experimental group of over one thousand college students. The intervention consisted of three identical writing assignments given to biology students several weeks before their unit tests. The prompt was as follows:

> Select a concept or issue that was covered in lecture and formulate a question. Select the relevant information from class notes and the textbook, and write a 1–2 page essay addressing this question and discuss the relevance of the concept or issue to your own life. Be sure to include some concrete information that was covered in this unit, explaining why this specific information is relevant to your life or useful for you. Be sure to explain how the information applies to you personally and give examples (p. 8).

In other words, students had to identify and explain concepts, issues, and information they learned about in class and how these concepts connected to things they valued in their own lives.

This assignment was only given three times, but the results were profound: Underrepresented students in the experimental group saw a 40 percent reduction in end-of-course achievement gaps; for first-generation underserved students, the gap reduction was an even greater 61 percent.

Powerfully, this intervention is far from a one-hit wonder in the research. In numerous randomized field trials, it's been found to

- increase short-term learning outcomes, including course-specific performance and interest;
- increase longer-term learning outcomes, such as course-taking and persistence in a major; and
- have a particularly strong effect for students at risk for poor performance, including students with a history of doing poorly in a course, students who indicate less confidence that they will do well in a course, and students from traditionally marginalized groups (Hulleman & Harackiewicz, 2020).

What I love about this kind of assignment is that it's good for all students to complete—just the content review opportunity alone is valuable to all learners. Think of the level of cognition required to consider content learned in a unit and apply that to one's life, values, or goals. And for students who entered class with Five Key Beliefs–related difficulties (e.g., low perceptions of subject Value or low perceptions of personal Efficacy for success in the course), it can prove *powerful* in altering trajectories.

To put it into practice in my classroom, I sometimes prompt my students with a writing assignment akin to that quoted above; other times, I frame this as a collaborative brainstorming activity. When my students walk in, they see simple instructions for their warm-up.

Warm-up

Today, I want you to make a T-chart, and we're going to do something we've done once beofe: build connections. On a fresh page of your spiral notebook, make a t-chart on the top half of the page.

COLUMN A:

On the left side of that T-chart, brainstorm a list of your interests, goals, and values.

COLUMN B:

On the right side, brainstorm a list of specific concepts or strategies you've learned in/from WH so far.

Goal: Ten items in each list

Now, very importantly, I don't just have students create these lists on their own. I have them put their pens in their hands, and then I talk them through different things they can write down. We start with Column A.

I say, "All right, so in the first column, we're going to write down things that you value. Let's start with your interests. When someone gives you free time to look things up on the Internet or you have free time at home, what activities and topics do you naturally go to? What topics do you like learning about on your own? What activities make you feel rested afterward or warm in your heart during?"

They snicker here. Good. They're listening.

"Now our goal here is to list five to ten things in Column A. So don't hold back! Just let the brainstorm come, and write things down. Let's look at goals you have for your life. What careers are you interested in? What are you hoping to do after high school? How about a family: Do you want one? What kind of family? What kind of friend do you want to be? Write down any words or phrases that describe this."

I'm walking around the room as I say this. If a student is stuck, I'll ask a quick and quiet direct question: "Psst, Morgen. If you could pick any job in the world after high school, what would it be? Write that down, man! That's something you value. That's great."

Then I say to the class, "All right, so now let's think about the qualities you'd like to be known for, the kind of person you'd like to be. If any of the words I'm saying resonate with you, write them down. How many of you want to be dependable—the kind of person that friends can count on? How many want to be strong—the kind that can weather good times and bad? How many want to be kind? Curious? Interesting? Fun? Hard-working?"[42]

Give one or two minutes for students to tap themselves out for Column A. I verbally emphasize throughout that a minimum goal is five interests, goals, or values (or if a lot of them are struggling, I'll say four or three) and that a stretch goal is ten.

---

[42] It's this last category—descriptors of the person I'd like to be—that I find very, very helpful with the rest of this activity. Go big on this. Ideally students will write three or four descriptors of the kind of person they'd like to be.

Next, I move on to Column B, narrating this one in a similar way. There are two things I want them to think about in this column: the *specific content* we've learned and the *general skills* we've had to practice in order to do the work of the class.

Then, we work at building our connections between the two lists. I tell the students to do the following:

- Draw lines between connected items in Columns A and B. "Aim for two to three connections," I instruct.

- Explain one connection with their partner during a brief Pair-Share conversation.

- Write out one connection. (I find that simple sentence templates such as "[Item from A] and [Item from B] are linked because _____" help students get started with the writing.)

- Share what they wrote with their partner.

I then call on several students to share with the class. Finally I have them write out an elaboration of the connection they've made. (Again, I like a template such as "[Item from B] could be important to my life because _____."

I find that it does take this level of coaching, at least initially, for my students to succeed at this activity. My ninth graders often especially need help thinking in terms of broad-level values and broad-level course skills—not just the content we're learning but the things we're doing with that content. I've found that it's pretty hard to connect world history content with one's values—not impossible, but hard— but it's pretty easy to connect the skills my course has students practice (studying, keeping track of assignments, doing homework, asking questions, pop-up debating) to the kinds of people they want to be.

Just like with all hard things I ask students to do, the goal of the first utility-value intervention exercise is for students to experience some success. From this humble foundation, an attentive teacher can build all kinds of beautiful things.

Try *Why* Conversations.

The only trouble with the utility-value intervention we just looked at is that it's pretty involved, requiring *at least* fifteen minutes of instructional time and *initially* even more than that. So while I do recommend that every teacher use the intervention based on its effectiveness in numerous studies, I think we need simpler and quicker methods to work with as well.

Why conversations are a perfect simplification. To initiate a *why* conversation, you basically just ask a student, or a small group of students, or a whole class of students to explain *why* the work you're doing in class is valuable in real life.

Just this morning, I did something like this with my students via the warm-up prompt below:

> A guy walks into our classroom and starts ranting about how world history[43] is a completely pointless class. "It's not worth studying, not worth the work." What do you say in response to his maniacal statements? What arguments do you bring against this naysayer?

Note that I'm being a bit playful with the language—I love doing that with students and find it to be an effective and fun method for encouraging their vocabulary development and writing sophistication—but at the core I'm just asking them to do what the utility-value intervention is doing: come up with connections between what we do *in this classroom* and what folks do *in real life*.

Here are some of the things my students came up with:[44]

- "I would say that this class doesn't teach us only about history but how to take notes, how to study, and more. For example, my notes at the beginning of the year were far worse than the notes I take now. Then, I would tell this naysayer that this class is important for college because it prepares me and shows me what a college class's work would roughly be like."

- "It's not pointless; it's a good way of challenging yourself. If someone says you shouldn't do it, it's also their opinion and doesn't matter to you. If you want to study and become more knowledgeable about history, then it's worth it. It's your decision at the end of the day, not theirs or anyone else's."

---

[43]You could incorporate your discipline with slight language modifications.

[44]I've made a few modifications to student submissions here for clarity's sake.

Value

- "Knowing and learning about more than just where you are in the world and seeing all the history is interesting and definitely worth studying and reading."
- "Well, it can help you get better at writing and reading, as well as note-taking."

This is the kind of thing I like to ask students to do some form of—via writing, or Pair-Share, or group discussion—once or so per month.

Ask Your Students to Find Your Discipline in the World.

Adam Craig is a math teacher in Massachusetts who gives his students the same homework assignment every weekend: Go find a "mathy moment." On Mondays, he asks his students to report on what they found.

Within a month or so, students in class will roll their eyes when one of their peers says, "I couldn't find one." They'll say things like, "C'mon, did you have to be anywhere on time? Did you buy something at a store? Did you alter your car's speed at a stoplight? Those are all mathy moments, dude!"

What I find genius about this "mathy moments" exercise is that students come to see that it's a very simple task. They see it as Mr. Craig showing them kindness over the weekend by giving them such a simple assignment. But in doing things this way, Mr. Craig is actually *being very sneaky* in training them to internalize that the Value of math is *everywhere*. It's all around us, and we use it all the time. It's central to life. That's a *master* move.

Effort and Efficacy

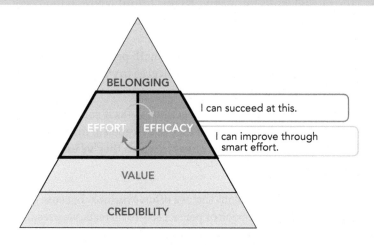

WHAT EFFORT AND EFFICACY ARE

WHAT **EFFORT** SOUNDS LIKE	WHAT **ANTI-EFFORT** SOUNDS LIKE	WHAT **EFFICACY** SOUNDS LIKE	WHAT **ANTI-EFFICACY** SOUNDS LIKE
I'm an improvementist.	I'm a perfectionist.	I can write one hundred words in response to a quick-write prompt.	There's no way I can write that much.
I'm a hard worker.	I'm smart.	I can master world history this year.	I've never been good at history.
I push myself in math.	I'm good at math.	I can learn physics.	I'm going to fail physics.
I like challenges.	I like things I know I'll succeed at.	I can get better at drawing this year in art class.	I can't draw.
Failure is my best teacher.	Failure terrifies me.	Chemistry doesn't make sense right now, but it will.	I just don't get chemistry.
If I'm to get better at this, it's up to me.	I can't get better at this.	I can turn my work in on time. I can stay organized.	I always turn things in late. Whenever I try getting organized, I always end up getting messy again. The same thing is going to happen this time.

Photo by Brooke Fournier

Let's begin with Effort. I think the most helpful avenue to help you interpret the Effort belief effectively is to talk to you about the many ways there are to misunderstand the role of Effort in improvement.

The Effort belief is absent when you don't think you can improve. Here we're talking about two kinds of students:

- those who think they're just "not a math person"—as if no degree of Effort can improve the degree to which they achieve or fail in math and

- those who think they're math geniuses—as if something inborn in them is the reason they are so good at math versus a trail of experiences in their lives in which they've undergone growth in mathematics.

It's this second kind of student that we often overlook. Because they tend to get As in the grade book or perfect scores on tests, we presume they are adequately motivated. But when a student thinks Effort is something detached from their ability to improve, make no mistake: that is a student inflicted with Effort unbelief.

Stanford's Carol Dweck calls this Effort unbelief a "false growth mindset." According to Dweck (2007), who popularized her career's research with the book *Mindset: The New Psychology of Success*, false growth mindset is something all of us struggle with, especially in circumstances where we

- are asked to work outside of our comfort zones,

- meet someone who is much better than us at something we previously thought we were very good at, or

- hit an obstacle that appears larger than our current ability to overcome it.

Effort & Efficacy

So, the Effort belief[45] is critical when students experience the kinds of challenges that best promote growth toward mastery.

So, too, is Efficacy. When a student encounters a growth-supportive challenge that seems bigger than their ability level, an internal check occurs: Can I do this? Will I come out on top? Can I succeed? It's like the sign before the rollercoaster line that asks, "Are you tall enough to ride this ride?" It's hard to overstate how powerfully our beliefs about our Efficacy predict our performance.

The best way to help students believe in their Efficacy is, of course, to help them to succeed at hard things. The proof, as they say, is in the pudding. When students succeed, they believe in their Efficacy; when they believe in their Efficacy, they are more likely to succeed. It's a bit of a chicken-or-egg paradox.

The Efficacy Paradox

SUCCESS

"I believe I can succeed."

SUCCESS

---

[45]Note that in Dweck's terminology, what I call the *Effort belief* is the same thing as what she calls *growth mindset* or, in her more technical writing, an *incremental theory of intelligence*. As I've said previously in this book, I find the term *belief* to be a more straightforward way to describe what Dweck and her colleagues are after with the term *mindset*. Being a psychologist, Dweck's work is rooted in the world of the mind, but being just an ordinary teacher, I can deal with human beings on their own terms, which seem to me to be the terms of the five-part soul, as we explored in Chapter 1.

In the front of my classroom hangs a sign that says, "Do hard things." I hang it there to remind both my students and myself that the things that we do are difficult yet attainable.

But if all I did was display that poster, it wouldn't do much for my students' Efficacy. Ultimately, for Efficacy to develop a student *must succeed*. This is why it's so important to teach students the steps to success for anything hard you're asking them to do (see Strategy 7), to define success in a manner that's attainable yet attractive for all students (see Strategy 8), and to unpack outcomes both good and bad so as to help students understand where success or failure comes from (see Strategy 9).

Now, having examined Effort and Efficacy separately, let's see how they play together. In the Five Key Beliefs model I've shared throughout this book, Effort and Efficacy circle one another. The reason for this is something that I call the Effort-Efficacy Flywheel. Basically, the Effort and the Efficacy beliefs feed into one another and, over time, can create a virtuous cycle. Like in an actual flywheel, momentum in these two beliefs breeds their further momentum.

The Effort-Efficacy Flywheel

students put forth **wise strategic effort**

students get **good results** from their efforts

students believe that **wise, strategic effort** pays off

Alternatively, of course, an inverse cycle can occur—we can call this the Effort-Efficacy Doom Loop.[46]

The Effort-Efficacy Doom Loop

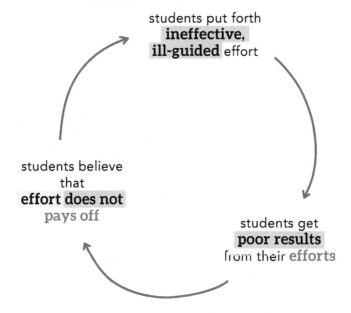

students put forth **ineffective, ill-guided** effort

students get **poor results** from their efforts

students believe that **effort does not** pays off

What we'd like to do in this section, then, is to remedy those spots in the loop that allow room for doom and strengthen them in order to create a virtuous, self-empowering flywheel. This is what Strategies 7, 8, and 9 will help us achieve.

COMMON TEACHER HANG-UPS

Oh, I've Heard About Growth Mindset.
Yeah, I'm a Growth Mindset Person.

There are two reasons I use the term *Effort belief* rather than *growth mindset*:

1. *Mindset* is a bad word to me. It gives too little acknowledgment to the human heart, will, and soul. We're not just minds.

(Continued)

---

[46]I first encountered this language for referring to an inverse flywheel in Collins's (2001) *Good to Great*.

(Continued)

2. *Growth mindset* is a term that everyone has heard of[47] but only a small sliver understands.

Let me explain that last claim. When her book was rocking the bestseller lists in the early 2010s, Carol Dweck started to notice a problem: Folks were speaking about growth mindset in ways that had no grounding in her research.

For one thing, Dweck noticed folks were discussing growth mindset as something you either have or you don't—more like an on/off switch in the head rather than a fluid belief that slides along a spectrum. "You hear a lot of people saying, 'I'm a growth mindset person'," Dweck (2018) said in an interview, but "it turns out that we're all a mixture, often depending on the environment we're in." Consider, she said, what happens to you when you encounter someone who is way better than you at something that you consider yourself good at: You experience doubt; your belief shifts. In other words, the Effort belief, like the rest of the Five Key Beliefs, is context-dependent—just as we said in Chapter 2.

Another misunderstanding with growth mindset is that to develop it in children, you must never call a child smart and you must always praise the process rather than the person. These maxims are drawn from sound research—for example, study participants have been found to succeed less when they're told that they're smart in a given area versus when they are told that they work hard in a given area—but they oversimplify the complex process of belief formation in a human soul.

Let's say you have a student who has worked very hard on a lab report in his science class, but the lab report is very bad. In this case, praising the process would be nonsensical—after all, the process did not work. Valorizing ineffective Effort sends a signal to students that school is a bizarre place where outcomes don't matter—all that matters is that you try. While such a world would perhaps have its perks, secondary students are savvy enough to

---

[47]In one study, over three-quarters of teachers indicated that they were very familiar with growth mindset (Clark & Soutter, 2022).

know that in other domains of life—sports, clubs, chores, jobs—it's not just Effort that matters. Outcomes matter, too.

All of which is to say that I recommend you clear your mind of what you think you know about growth mindset before moving further into this chapter. Think only of this: How am I demonstrating for students that effective Effort can pay off? How am I making effective Effort clear? How am I designing challenges so that they are attainable to my students but also challenging across the wide spectrum of my students' ability levels?

Not easy questions, are they? Yet they are critical.

My Students Won't Do Anything.

When you have a student who refuses to do anything, you must first depersonalize the situation and then ask yourself a few targeted questions.

First of all, remember: What happens in our classrooms isn't about our internal worth. We can't take demotivation personally. It serves no good end. That established, here are a few questions to ask yourself:

- Have I made the work clear? Have I broken the work down into its smallest chunks? Strategy 7 helps with this.
- Have I demonstrated to students that I care about them, academically *and* personally? Strategy 1 helps here.
- Have I sought to winsomely and confidently "make the case" for this work? That's Strategy 4.
- Is the work appropriately challenging for this student? Not too easy *and* not too hard? If it's not, what are the simplest means through which I could remedy this?

Through it all, keep this one idea in mind: All human beings *want* to be motivated. This student does, too. There's just something getting in the way right now—something that you get to work at puzzling out.

(Continued)

(Continued)

My Students Are Working Hard, but Their Work Isn't Paying Off.

A student walks up to you and says, "Ms. Smith, I don't get it!" There are tears in her eyes. "I studied for five hours last night, and then today on the test I still failed it. Argh!"

This is such an important situation that we're going to deal with it at length in Strategy 9: Unpack Outcomes, Good or Bad on page 206.

Strategy 7: Woodenize All of It

While producing what became the best decade of performance in the history of sports, UCLA coach John Wooden famously began each basketball season teaching his players how to put on their socks and shoes. The instruction was explicit; he included statements like "You must not permit your socks to have wrinkles around the little toe—where you generally get blisters—or around the heels" (Gordon, 1999). He even used step-by-step modeling:

> Hold up the sock, work it around the little toe area and the heel area so that there are no wrinkles. Smooth it out good. Then hold the sock up while you put the shoe on. And the shoe must be spread apart—not just pulled on the top laces. You tighten it up snugly by each eyelet. Then you tie it. And then you double-tie it so it won't come undone. (Gordon, 1999)

It's this picture—an older adult explicitly teaching and modeling for younger adults how to do something they had learned to do as small children—that I want in your mind as we approach this strategy. If we expect our students to do something, we must teach them—all of them—how best to do it.

How Strategy 7 Influences the Five Key Beliefs

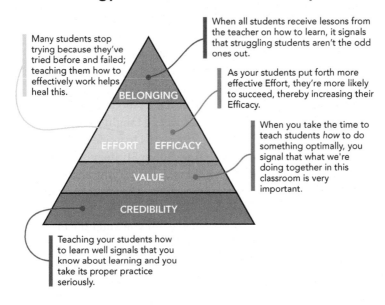

Many students stop trying because they've tried before and failed; teaching them how to effectively work helps heal this.

When all students receive lessons from the teacher on how to learn, it signals that struggling students aren't the odd ones out.

As your students put forth more effective Effort, they're more likely to succeed, thereby increasing their Efficacy.

When you take the time to teach students *how* to do something optimally, you signal that what we're doing together in this classroom is very important.

Teaching your students how to learn well signals that you know about learning and you take its proper practice seriously.

BELONGING

EFFORT   EFFICACY

VALUE

CREDIBILITY

Effort & Efficacy

What to Do

- If there is a learning-conducive behavior that you know helps students progress more effectively up the mountain path to mastery, then you absolutely, positively, without a doubt must teach, model, and reinforce it—no matter how small or big the behavior is.

- Think in terms of two categories of behavior:
  - smallies (e.g., writing your name on your paper, uppercasing the first-person pronoun *I*) and
  - biggies (e.g., taking notes, studying, listening, speaking).

Key Pointer

- Every learning-conducive behavior needs to be taught as briefly as possible, as frequently as needed, and in a way that supports a student's sense of worth and dignity.

WHY THIS STRATEGY

Why Wooden?

First, let's cover a few reasons why Mr. John Wooden gets a strategy named after him.

- Wooden's first lesson of the basketball season—how to put on your socks and tie your shoes—is a striking parable for just what we're after in this strategy. We want to assume nothing and teach everything, from things as simple as writing your name on the top of your paper to actions as complex as studying effectively. Like Wooden, we teach these things as quickly as they can be taught because our job isn't to be a minutiae teacher—it's to guide students toward mastery of a discipline. But in Strategy 7, we clothe ourselves with Wooden's genius insight: Tying shoes was "just a little detail that coaches must take advantage of, because it's the little details that make the big things come about" (Gordon, 1999). Colleague, for you and I the big thing is motivated movement toward mastery. And teaching even the little things helps.

- Furthermore, John Wooden did not consider his career as having been that of a coach. He began his career in 1934 as an English teacher at South Bend Central High School in Indiana—this was long before he would become a household name during what many commentators call the greatest coaching career in history. During all of this, Wooden thought of himself as an *educator*. In his own words: "In the eyes of most observers, my title is 'Coach' Wooden, but this is not what I would list first on my résumé or business card. From my earliest years I have viewed my primary job as one of educating others: I am a teacher" (Wooden, 2005, p. 92).

- Wooden, as a teacher, embodied not just instruction and practice but also love. His players uniformly recall him as a source of wisdom, guidance, and support. At the time of his death in 2010, former player Bill Walton shared remarks like this one: "The joy and happiness in Coach Wooden's life came from the success and accomplishments of others. He never let us forget what he learned from his two favorite teachers, Abraham Lincoln and Mother Teresa, that 'a life not lived for others is not a life.'"

Before we move on from Mr. Wooden, I want to return once more to this idea of assumptions that I mentioned a moment ago. Wooden was teaching young men who, by the time they arrived at UCLA as college freshmen, had clearly indicated advanced mastery of basketball. So his socks-and-shoes lesson is an effective picture of how explicit and foundational we aim to be here. Just as Wooden didn't assume all of his college players could effectively put on their socks and tie their shoes, you and I ought not to assume that our secondary students know how to take notes (see pages 184–189), study, focus, improve their handwriting, complete a warm-up, or avoid distracting writing errors (see pages 189–191).

What Kinds of Strategies Should We Explicitly Teach, Model, and Reinforce?

Many secondary schools are plagued with a bad notion: Study strategies are the kinds of things that you teach only in a study skills or advisory class. They are not the kinds of things that ought to be embedded throughout the school day, the reasoning goes; instead, students just ought to know how to do these things.

This idea isn't just bad, it's destructive. In an influential paper for *Scientific American*, a panel of cognitive scientists concluded that, despite having clear evidence that some learning strategies help students a lot and others don't help at all, "this information is not making its way into the classroom" (Dunlosky et al., 2015). "In fact," the researchers said, "the two study aids that students rely on the most are not effective."

The two study aids most *supported* by the researchers in this paper, by the way, are not complex; they could be taught by any secondary teacher who gives tests of any kind. They are self-quizzing aids, such as flashcards, sample questions, and Cornell notes, and distributed practice, in which students spread their studying across multiple days instead of cramming.

Not exactly rocket science, is it? Yet, due to their being woefully under-taught and reinforced in secondary schools, the researchers found that instead of using these highly effective, practical, and efficient strategies, most of the students they surveyed relied instead on highlighting and re-reading. These are often *worse* than time-wasters—they can actually *undermine* student achievement because they trick students into thinking they know more than they know. For example, think of the last time a student showed you his elaborately highlighted textbook. The student likely felt proud and confident because of the time spent on the page doing the highlighting. The trouble, however, is that unless the student quizzes himself on the knowledge contained on the page, he is likely to have only achieved a *familiarity* with the *page*—not a *mastery* of the *content*.

So, if there were just two strategies I would ask all secondary teachers to Woodenize, I guess it would be self-quizzing and distributed practice. But the brilliance of John Wooden isn't that he's teaching the most high-impact behaviors to his students; it's that he's teaching *all* behaviors to his students. Even socks and shoes. So if there's *anything* that you'd like your students to know or get better at, then you must explicitly teach them, just as Wooden did with shoe-tying. You must teach exactly the best way(s) in which the thing can be done. If it's worth your students doing, then it's worth you teaching, modeling, and reinforcing. That's the idea beneath Strategy 7.

What Happens When You Don't Teach Wise Effort?

The fundamental act of Strategy 7 is that we're making *wise* Effort clear. We want our students not just to work *hard*; we want to empower them to work *smart*.

During the heyday of growth mindset—which is really what my Effort belief is; I've just renamed it because of how much misunderstanding there is around growth mindset—Carol Dweck started noticing a key problem: Parents and teachers were praising students for hard work even when the hard work was ineffective.

While this may seem like a nice thing to do, it's actually deeply damaging to the Effort belief. Students *want* to be successful; they *want* their efforts to pay off. And when they don't but the adults they trust are nonetheless praising them for working hard, they become disoriented. School becomes this weird place where the adults see a reality that is undetectable to the students. To the students, it seems like things would be better if their efforts paid off, but this praise-for-efforts-regardless-of-outcome seems to be painting a picture of a whole different and weird way of seeing things.

The best remedies for this problem, thankfully, are Strategies 7, 8, and 9:

- We teach students how to work not just hard but smart (Strategy 7).

- We guide students to define success realistically and holistically (Strategy 8).

- We unpack outcomes with students so that they can reflect and improve upon their work in the future (Strategy 9).

The best thing I can do for you here is give you a couple examples of what it looks like in my ninth-grade classroom when I implement Strategy 7: Woodenize All of It.

Before we do that, I think it's helpful to break up the total list of behaviors that we're going to try to teach into two categories: biggies and smallies.

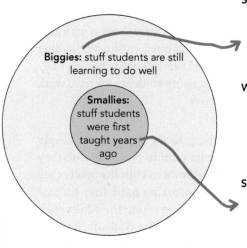

Some examples of biggies:

- taking notes that help you learn
- studying effectively
- focusing

What teachers should do:

- Teach, model, and share examples and nonexamples and reinforce *over time* (these are not one-and-done lessons)

Some examples of smallies:

- write legibly
- capitalize first-person pronoun *I*
- complete the warm-up

What teachers should do:

Teach, model, and share examples and nonexamples in one brief-and-direct-as-possible mini-lesson, then reinforce as students are going about the rest of the semester (e.g., do not allow lowercased *i*)

Biggies are the kinds of skills that are properly on the growth threshold of your students. What I mean is that for my ninth graders, for example, I don't expect that they've mastered taking notes on course material in a way that is both efficient and helpful. Nor do I expect that they've mastered how to synthesize and study course material at the high school level. Because of this, I expect to need to teach, model, reinforce, and provide examples and nonexamples repeatedly throughout the school year. I'll need to observe how they are doing and adjust my instruction accordingly.

In short, biggies are the learning behaviors that can't be taught just once. Smallies, on the other hand, can be taught just once *so long as* they are strictly reinforced thereafter.

Picture John Wooden's shoe-tying example. It would be silly for Wooden to teach this more than one time. All he would need to do after this brief lesson is consistently react to any instances of poor shoe tying that he saw thereafter. If a player's shoe became unlaced during practice, Wooden would only need to walk up to the player and say, "Hello. Did you double knot your shoes? Make sure to always do that. I don't want you getting hurt or wasting your practice time with shoe tying."

That small bit of reinforcement applied in 100 percent of circumstances is where the power of the mini-lesson for a smallie comes in. To bring it back to our classrooms, many of our students have been taught that they need to capitalize the first-person pronoun *I*. The reason they often don't do this is not a matter of not having been taught; it's a matter of not having been given robot-like reinforcement of the habit.

I like to remind my students that the smallies I teach them are the kinds of behaviors that they learned many years prior but perhaps have failed to fully habituate or apply. I share with them that because I also have a few poor habits I sometimes need to address. I promise I will help them to establish good and simple habits during their time with me.

Before I unpack our biggie and smallie examples, here's how I recommend that you get started with Strategy 7 in your practice. The following steps can be very enjoyable to complete and discuss as a department or professional learning community (PLC) as well.

Step 1: Brainstorm a list of learning-conducive behaviors you would like all students to do well. (It may be helpful to differentiate between smallies and biggies here.) Here are some examples I've heard from teachers around the country when we brainstorm lists like this during my workshops.

SMALLIES	BIGGIES
(TEACH ONCE, THEN REINFORCE CONSISTENTLY.)	(TEACH, MODEL, AND REINFORCE ON AN ONGOING BASIS.)
• Stretching in phys ed	• Shooting a free throw in phys ed
• Tuning your instrument in band	• Staying organized
• Writing your name on your paper	• Prioritizing
• Coming into the classroom and getting started with the warm-up	• Asking questions when confused (or even knowing how to know *when* you are confused)
• Sharpening your pencil	• Collaborating with classmates
• Coming to class prepared	• Managing your time
• Minimizing distractions	• Thinking before you speak
• Improving handwriting	• Reading independently
• Speaking audibly	• Communicating effectively
• Entering and exiting the room with consideration for others	• Working as a team
• Leaving your space like you found it (or better)	• Holding yourself accountable
• Submitting an assignment when you finish it	• Studying effectively
	• Identifying confusion and asking questions
	• Taking risks
	• Receiving feedback effectively

Step 2: For each item on your list, brainstorm some or all of the following:

- A sequence of steps for completing the behavior effectively

- A list of pointers for completing the behavior effectively

- A list of examples and nonexamples you could use, curate, or create to help students clearly conceive of what it does and doesn't look like to complete the behavior

- Method(s) you could use for reinforcing the behavior over time (be biased toward simplicity here; see my Skull and Crossbones example on page 189)

- The winsome and sure apologetic (Strategy 4) for this behavior; in other words, how could you answer your students' questions about why they have to learn something?

That's really it! Now let's exemplify the Woodenization process with how I teach a biggie and a smallie in my classroom.

Where to Woodenize

Warm-up	• students working independently • teacher attempting an MGC • teacher completing admin tasks
Lesson intro/ go over warm-up	• teacher or students provide lesson rationale • students share warm-up work • teacher gives whole-class feedback
Lesson chunk 1	• students read or listen to a knowledge-rich text • teacher provides direct instruction and guided practice • teacher models how to put forth wise effort in learning
Lesson chunk 2	• students read or listen to a knowledge-rich text • teacher provides direct instruction and guided practice • teacher models how to put forth wise effort in learning
Lesson chunk 3	• students read or listen to a knowledge-rich text • teacher provides direct instruction and guided practice • teacher models how to put forth wise effort in learning
Tie it all together	• teacher leads reflective application of today's lesson • students make connections
Closing	• teacher gives mini-sermon on value of lesson students engage in engaging retrieval practice (e.g., Quizlet, Kahoot, Gimkit, Blooket)

I like to use *one* of these 12–15 minute lesson chunks for Woodenizing something; this allows the remainder of the lesson chunks to be spent on instruction and practice directly related to my discipline.

This is a good place to remind students that we studied not just our discipline today but also how better to learn it.

Biggie Example: Take Notes for Learning

One school year when we were about five weeks into the first semester, I gave my students the following post-assessment reflection[48] prompt: What's one piece of evidence that you can find from your life during Unit 2 that demonstrates that you are making progress in your growth as a learner?

Here's some of what they shared:

- "I can find one piece of evidence that I am progressing as a learner by looking at my notes. I finally found a way that works for me and is efficient when it comes to taking notes and understanding it all a whole lot better."

- "During Unit Two, I got a lot faster at taking notes. Week by week, I get faster, and I take notes more efficiently. I went from sixty-plus minutes to thirty-five minutes at most."

- "I get my notes done faster. I am better at deciphering whether the information is worthy of being written down or not."

- "I've been a lot more efficient in my homework during Unit 2, which has helped me to grow as a learner. I haven't been stressing as much about homework and schoolwork, so I've been able to stop procrastinating and get my work done."[49]

As I read those, here's what I registered as super promising:

- My students were prizing efficiency.

- They were actively thinking about what they were learning while taking notes—for example, according to one student, "I am better at deciphering whether the information is worthy of being written down."

- They were internalizing the conjoined goals of *more learning* and *less stress*.

These are all things that I want for my students because they will maximize their mastery of my course material. Now let's look at what brought us to that reflection activity.

---

[48]This is one of the methods we'll explore in Strategy 9 on page 206.

[49]I love that this student sees the link between stress and performance.

Start by doing. At the start of the year, I just had students take notes one night—no instruction. I gave them five or so pages of reading and said, "Take notes on these. Aim to be done in thirty to forty-five minutes."

The next morning, I woke up to more than a handful of e-mails from students saying that they had been in tears doing the notes. It was super overwhelming, it took them two-plus hours, etc.

Now we had a baseline.

Set a time limit. That day in class I asked students how the notes had gone, and they mostly said, "Not great. It was overwhelming. It was stressful. I cried."

I responded, "All right. I don't want that to happen to any of you again. From now on, I need you to try to learn everything you can from me about taking notes. You all have different lives and different constraints, and you'll be working *with* those—not against them—to find a note-taking method that works for you."

"Right now," I continued, "tell your partner about how much time you have on a normal weeknight to give to this class."

After they had done this, I said, "All right. Unless you are obsessively in love with this class material, I want all of you to allot forty-five minutes *max* for this class each night. Our job in the next few weeks will be figuring out how to get there."

Let the modeling begin. From this point on, I'm not going to go more than one day of class without modeling note-taking for my students. This means that five weeks into the school year, my students and I have taken notes together about twenty times. This is part of why so many of them are so clear on how to take notes successfully.

Modeling is one of the great secrets of teaching. It makes the abstract concrete. It is also remarkably easy from the teacher's point of view. I just find a video on YouTube or a brief text excerpt, fire up my doc camera, and together my students and I take notes. As we're doing that, I talk through everything I'm doing and thinking as I take notes.

Assign the thirty-minute challenge. A week or so into teaching and modeling note-taking, I still have students who are spending sixty-plus minutes on note-taking at home. By this point, they're asking me if they should drop my class. But they are the exact opposite of people who should drop my class—they're hard-working but prone to stress. I've got something that will help.

When introducing the coming night's homework, I tell them all, "Look. Tonight we have one rule when taking notes. None of you are allowed to take more than thirty minutes. I need you to set a timer on your phone, and if you don't trust yourself to obey the timer, I need you to have a parent or guardian keep time for you. And while you're taking notes, just keep an eye on that timer. Your goal is to get through all the reading before the timer ends."

I tell them they'll need to

- be strategic and picky about what they write down,
- make the text's author their partner—use the author's headings and organizational structures—not their adversary,
- smile because this is a fun challenge, and
- give themselves some grace.

I tell them, "The worst thing that can happen tonight is you don't get all the way done with the reading before the timer goes off. That's fine. Shut the book, shut your spiral notebook, and go do something else. We'll unpack it all tomorrow."

The next day we process how it went. During the warm-up, the students write reflectively about it, then they talk with a partner. After this, volunteers share with the whole class. It's a really fun conversation—light bulbs are starting to flicker on. I hear, "Ooooooohhhhh . . . I don't have to perfectly comprehend *everything* I'm taking notes on! Learning is a process! And I can take a hard class and still have a life!"

Teach basic note-taking conventions. Whenever I take notes, I've got the title of the page up at the top and the source of the notes in a box in the upper-right corner.

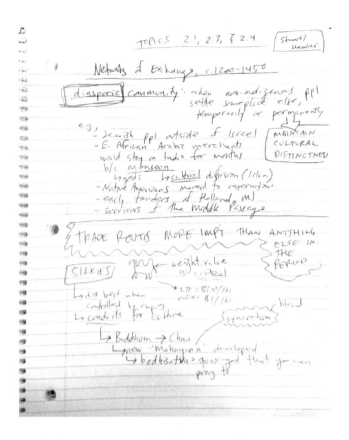

I explain to students that I'm not doing this because I'm "supposed to." I'm doing this as a favor to future me.

Ask: Who is the reader of these notes? I ask my students often in those first weeks, "Who is the reader of your notes? Who are you writing these for?" By default, most of them unconsciously assume that when a teacher assigns note-taking, that means that they are taking notes for the teacher. Asking them this question helps them to unearth the obvious answer: "I'm taking these for me."

Once they come to this realization, I say, "So, in terms of legibility, it needs to be readable to us. This isn't a license for sloppiness, but it should help us relax a bit. In terms of abbreviations and symbols, the reader is us—this lets us be creative a bit. In terms of drawings, sketches, and diagrams—again, they're for us. We don't need to be artistic. We just need to learn."

Ask: What is the point of note-taking? We take notes for one reason: to learn. We learn while we take notes, we learn as we ask questions during the note-taking process, and we learn later on when we quiz ourselves with our notes.

We take notes so we can re-read them to quiz ourselves. Re-reading is the bane of a student's existence. It is the epitome of wasting time. Re-reading produces a dreaded relationship with content: familiarity. Familiarity is that cursed feeling you get during a test where you say, "Oh shoot—I know this! Why can't I think of it right now? I'm blanking out!" Familiarity is not the same thing as knowing.

To make sure that we know something, the only thing to do is to quiz ourselves. We can do this in a couple of ways:

- We can cover up portions of our past notes and try to verbally recount what we've covered up—for instance, we might ask ourselves, "What are three examples of syncretism from 1200–1450? How did these mergings happen?"

- We can do a quick skim of a past page of notes then close our notebook and pretend that we are giving a mini-lecture to our classmates *on the page*. This means lots of explaining and illustration; this means making clear key terms and ideas. After the mini-lecture, take a look at the page again and highlight anything you forgot to mention. Try the same thing again the next day.

Ask your teacher. I'm never trying to hide the ball from my students. If they ask me, "Hey, Mr. Stuart, is _____ important from last night's reading?" I'll say, "Good on ya" for asking that question and then share my thought process on why it is or isn't important. (Note that I've got to keep these explanations brief in order to keep my students' attention—quick questions want quick answers.)

Think in terms of drafts of learning. One important moment occurs when my students understand that the reading they're doing at night isn't going to be used for some kind of "gotcha" the next day. Instead, the next day we'll write about what we read, discuss it, watch another teacher's take on it via YouTube (and take notes on that take), or have a pop-up debate.

I tell them often that when I assign work for home, that isn't the last time we'll look at that work. It's the first. I expect them to do what they can to begin learning the new material. And then I'll be a good partner in helping them to take it deeper.

That's about it. If I'm going to teach my students to do something, I need to understand how that something works. At this point in my career, I get why note-taking matters in a class like AP world history, and I see that there are many things note-taking can teach us about life.

I really do believe that teaching students toward academic mastery is the perfect context within which to teach them about life.

Smallie Example: How to Capitalize the First-Person Pronoun *I*

Like with all smallies, secondary students learn how to do this one when they are very young in school. And while I often hear teachers say things like, "Well, with texting today, it just is what it is—students don't capitalize things like they used to," I don't see how growing up texting means that you can't capitalize every single ever-loving first-person pronoun that you write in school. Here's how I approach this.

First, I teach the Skull and Crossbones. Just after my students have completed their warm-up for the lesson, I ask them to get out their spiral notebooks and label a fresh page "Skull and Crossbones."[50] I invite them to go ahead and draw one too, if they'd like. As they're doing this, I'm also preparing a fresh page in my spiral notebook up on the document camera, drawing the best little skull and crossbones figure that I can muster.

I then begin instructing:

"All right—so what is the deal with this Skull and Crossbones idea in my classroom? It's simply this. There are some bad habits that I notice ninth graders can have when it comes to basic writing rules that you learned back in second grade or so. I'm not judging or trying to be offensive when I say that—we all can get into bad habits that go against what we know. It's part of being human; it just is what it is.

---

[50]This strategy is treated at greater length in my book *These 6 Things: How to Focus Your Teaching on What Matters Most* (2018).

"Part of my job as your teacher this year is to teach you as if you were my very own children. And one thing that I would not allow my very own children to do is to keep going with some of these bad writing habits.

"Today, I want to introduce just one: the lowercased first-person pronoun *i*. Let's write this down, along with a good and a bad example of what we're talking about.

"So, you know how to do this correctly, right? But, if we're being honest, how many of you sometimes don't capitalize this little guy? Yes, yes—look around. You're not alone.

"But from now on when you submit a piece of writing for me to read—during a warm-up, as part of an assessment, in an essay—any time that I see the lowercased first person *i*, I'll just mark a skull and crossbones on your paper or an emoji skull on your document and I'll return it back to you. When you see that skull and crossbones, you'll know what you need to do: Take a look through your work for any error that we've recorded on this page of your spiral notebook, fix the error(s), and resubmit the writing for no penalty.

"To close, let me restate that the reason I do things like this is because I value you as a human being and I respect your mind and your work. My goal is to teach you as if you were my own. I appreciate you very much."

Afterwards, I reinforce it every time I see it. There are two situations in which I reinforce the Skull and Crossbones list.

I. When students submit work and I see a Skull and Crossbones problem, I do as I said I would do in the instructions above. It is sometimes tempting to ignore little errors like this for the sake of avoiding the added layer of now needing to return a student's work to them. But the key to this method working is reinforcing it 100 percent of the time.

2. When students are writing in class and I am reading over their shoulders, if I see a Skull and Crossbones error, I say something immediately. "Oh—there's a Skull and Crossbones problem there. Take a look at that and give it a fix." Sometimes it's helpful for me to gently smile while I'm saying this so as to sound a bit warmer than I might otherwise.

And that's that. This eradicates 98 percent of lowercased *i* problems in my classroom.

COMMON TEACHER HANG-UPS

I Don't Know the Best Way for My Students to Do *X* Learning Behavior. How Am I Supposed to Pretend That I Do?

Don't pretend. Learn!

- At your next department meeting, ask the team, "Does anyone have a good method they teach students for *X*?"
- Google your question with a query like, "What is the best way to *X*?" You'll need to sift for quality, but it's likely that the first page of results will return some gems. You may even be able to excerpt something that you find and give it to your students as an article to read and annotate at the start of your next class.
- Search your query on YouTube. As with a Google result, an excerpt from the video may serve well as a resource when teaching your students the behavior you're after.
- Find your nerdiest colleague and ask them if they've come across any tips for *X* in the professional literature.

And hey, have *fun* learning this stuff! You'll use it all the rest of your career.

(Continued)

(Continued)

How Am I Supposed to Teach One Way of Doing Something When My Students Are Individuals or There Are So Many Good Ways to Do Something?

You don't need to sell your way as *the only way* to complete a learning behavior. But it's not a waste of time for you to arrive at a settled sense of what you've noticed works best for students. Remember, your students have lots of teachers. They've had lots before you. They'll have lots more after. You don't need to be the end-all, be-all teacher for them. But what you *do* need to be is someone who is knowledgeable about how learning works best in a class like yours.

After all, if your students do get lots of different examples in their education of how to take notes, is that such a bad thing? Just think back to that Purdie and Hattie (2002) study, which we discussed on page 115. The more conceptions of learning that the students in the study had—e.g., learning is taking in new information, learning is developing oneself, etc—the more likely they were to do well in school. In short, there is some benefit to students being taught multiple ways to do things.

At the same time, research in cognitive science is far enough along to where we do know that *some* strategies and methods just don't work well. For example, at the start of this strategy, we touched on students' overreliance on ineffective study methods such as re-reading and highlighting. A teacher would be remiss, then, to teach students that the best way to study is by re-reading the text.

Another example of this would be teaching students to let their learning styles guide their study methods. Despite decades of studies, learning style theory—the idea that if students are

---

[51] I know this single paragraph is likely to make at least a few readers think I've gone bonkers. For an excellent explanation of learning style theory's lack of support in the research, see Willingham's (2017) blog entry (with links to published articles) titled, "How Many People Believe Learning Styles Theories Are Right? And Why?"

allowed to learn according to their learning styles they will achieve more than if they are required to learn some other way—has yet to be empirically corroborated. Because of this I do not recommend teaching learning style theory to students.[51]

Why Is It My Job to Teach These Things?
I've Already Got Enough on My Plate.

When I teach Strategy 7 to groups of colleagues, I sometimes hear pushback to the tune of, "Oh great—here's *another* thing being added to my plate. How typical."

I do get the sentiment. As a classroom-based plate-holder myself, I too have spent time feasting at the more-than-you-can-eat initiatives buffet. However, I don't think Woodenize All of It is this kind of a thing.

What we're doing with Woodenization is, in the long run, making our jobs much easier and simpler as teachers. Just consider: How much time have you spent in your career remedying situations that would have never arisen had students just done the things that you asked them to do? Revised their papers, turned in their assignments, kept unit objectives organized, turned in the permission slip, written their name on their papers—how much time?

What we're after when we Woodenize All of It is the same thing John Wooden was after: For the small price of five minutes of instruction and relentless reinforcement thereafter, Wooden likely never dealt with players who became injured or ineffective due to ill-fitting shoes. And even more than this, Wooden signalled something to his players each time that he taught things like shoe-tying (a smallie) or how to pass a basketball (a biggie): "I know what I'm doing. I care about your success. I'll leave nothing to chance. And on this team, our efforts *will* pay off—you can count on it."

Strategy 8: Define Success Wisely, Early, and Often

When we don't define success for our students and guide them to define success for themselves, most of us end up frustrated. Some students define success as something unattainably beyond them; for example, the student who struggles academically defining success as all As, or the student with a C average defining success as 100 percent on tests. This isn't helpful for them or for us, and it makes the Efficacy belief all but impossible to cultivate.

The solution, thankfully, isn't that complicated. We need to give students regular, robust opportunities to contemplate success in our classes, in school, and in life.

What to Do

- **Think in timescales.** Ask yourself: What's success for this activity, this lesson, this unit, this entire course?

- **Think beyond your course.** Ask: What's a successful year look like for my students? A successful career at my middle or high school? A successful next decade of their life? A successful lifetime?

- **Emphasize toward.** Schools exist to help students flourish long-term by means of advancing them toward mastery. *Toward mastery.* That's what each class is for—moving students toward mastery, whether it be of drawing or running the mile or understanding biology or explicating poems.

- **Be the leader.** How can you embody this *toward* ethos for your students? How can you do this both within school and without?

Key Pointer

Don't do it just once! Strong, vibrant, well-founded internal definitions come from repeated exposure to and reflection on a concept. Students need many chances in each of their classes to think on what they're after and how they'll know that they've achieved it.

How Strategy 8 Influences the Five Key Beliefs

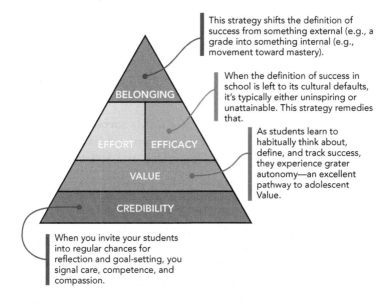

This strategy shifts the definition of success from something external (e.g., a grade into something internal (e.g., movement toward mastery).

When the definition of success in school is left to its cultural defaults, it's typically either uninspiring or unattainable. This strategy remedies that.

As students learn to habitually think about, define, and track success, they experience grater autonomy—an excellent pathway to adolescent Value.

When you invite your students into regular chances for reflection and goal-setting, you signal care, competence, and compassion.

Perhaps our most damaging fiction in American secondary schooling is that human success can be standardized. Try though we may, it resists singleton definitions or benchmarks. The trouble with success—and therefore Efficacy—is that success is so often subjective.

It's just a dodgy word—especially when you consider how infrequently our secondary students tend to get to think on success and hear it clearly communicated. For most of our students, success in school is left undefined and unreflected upon. As a result, Efficacy—the belief that one can succeed—almost surely suffers.

The dictionary, as so happens, does not offer us much help. It returns some derivation on "achieving one's desired aim"—which is subjective. And the culture, of course, is also not helpful. Success is having a million social media followers, or fame, or fortune. It is a professional athlete's abilities or a multi-platinum musician's

Effort & Efficacy

acumen. All things, it turns out, that are defined by the rareness with which they're reached.

It is this dilemma—that success is often ill-defined in a student's heart or not defined at all—that Strategy 8 will seek to remedy.

Strategy 8 relies on two components for its successful execution: definitions of success generated and communicated by teachers and definitions of success generated and reflected upon by students.

Two Approaches to Efficacy Cultivation in the Classroom

iStock.com/blyjak

Teacher-generated definitions of success

- generating is more in your control
- likelihood of your efforts succeeding long term is lower

(you want to use both)

Student-generated definitions of success

- generating is less in your control
- likelihood of your efforts succeeding long term is higher

This should look familiar to you as it's the same binary proposition that I made when discussing the best approach to cultivating Value in the classroom.

First, Make Sure You're Clear on Success Yourself.

If the teacher's not clear, there's little chance that the students will be. Start with this idea: Student success is movement toward mastery of your discipline or art.

That word *toward* is the key. I partnered with a junior high school in the Salt Lake City area once, and while we were doing a professional development session on this strategy, principal Diane Wanamaker summed it all up in that one word: *toward*. It goes all the way back to page one of this book: Schools exist to promote the long-term flourishing of young people by teaching them *toward* mastery of disciplines and arts that they may not get a chance to master outside of school.

With *toward* in mind, then, let's move forward.

Regularly Ask Your Students to Define Success in Your Class.

These are the kinds of questions I like to ask my students:

- What's success look like for you this school year? What's a reasonable and specific and meaningful goal that you have for yourself this school year?

- What kind of person do you want to be one day? What could you do this [lesson, week, unit, semester] to work toward becoming that person? How could success in this class contribute to your long-term success as an individual?

- Fill in the blanks: Lots of people my age talk about success as if it's just about _____. For me, however, it's more about _____.

These are not fancy questions. But, when asked regularly—during warm-ups, during lesson chunk transitions, at the end of class—they begin to shape your students' definitions of success into something far more likely to be both attainable (Efficacy) and meaningful (Value).

Once in a While, Have Your Students Do Some GOOP.

All right, I'll admit it—it's supposed to be WOOP, not GOOP. This idea comes from German psychologist Gabrielle Oettingen's famous WOOP interventions, in which she asked study participants to work through the following goal-setting steps:

1. Wish (or, to make it GOOP, Goal): What's a specific, measurable, time-sensitive goal you'd like to accomplish?

2. Outcome: Visualize and imagine what it would be like to achieve that goal. What good things could come of it? How would you feel? Who would you excitedly tell?

3. Obstacle: Visualize and imagine the you-based obstacles most likely to get in the way of your success. By "you-based" I mean an obstacle that is firmly within your realm of agency. For example, for me trying to stay consistent on a new diet, the obstacle is, "I go to bed without preparing for tomorrow's meals," rather than, "I have to attend a birthday party and there is ice cream there." For a student who wants to study for a big exam for twenty minutes per day for the next two weeks, the obstacle is, "I mismanage my time," not, "I have chores to do."

4. Plan: Create a simple if-then plan that could help you overcome the obstacle you just envisioned. For example, if I'm at a birthday party and there's ice cream, then I'll pull out the baggie of almond slivers I keep in my back pocket and snack on those instead of ice cream.[52]

To make your in-class GOOPs particularly good, here are a few extra pointers:

- Frame them with your students as experiments in success. You want your students to experience goal-setting as something pleasurable, therefore it needs to not be too over- or underpressured in their hearts.

- The entire GOOP-setting process does not take that long. In ten minutes or so, you can guide a class through it. This makes it easy to incorporate into your class once a month or so.

- You can focus GOOPs how you prefer. You can have students GOOP for a unit you are starting in your class, or for a new semester they are beginning in school, or for

---

[52]To be clear, this is hypothetical. I rarely carry almond slivers in my back pocket. But I could, couldn't I? And that's the point of the planning phase of GOOP—doing something about those obstacles.

something unrelated to school that they care about. All of these have benefits for the overarching goal of Strategy 8, which is to have them grow more thoughtful and wise about success.

- Sometimes I ask students to input their goals into a Google Doc. This allows me to follow up with them after a week or two or three and ask how things are going. (This follow-up can even be an MGC attempt—see Strategy 1.)

Want to Deepen the Impact? Have Them GOOP for a Month.

Once in a while, I'll work to budget a bit of time for four Mondays in a row so that we can do a month of GOOPing. Here's how it works:

- On the first Monday, I guide students through the GOOP process, telling them that the goal part needs to be something that can be completed between now and the next Monday. I typically allow students to set up to three goals of their choosing, and I encourage them to think both academically and personally.

- On the following Monday, we go through the following protocol in partners:

  1. I have students share with their partner what their goal was and how it went. I tell them to try to remain speaking for a full sixty seconds. (I keep time for the students and frame this as a Conversation Challenge; many of my students struggle to hold the floor in a classroom-based conversation for a full sixty seconds.)

  2. After both students have shared, I have both set a new goal. Here I lead them through a GOOP.

  3. Finally, I have them share with their partner what their new goal is and why it's important to them. Again, I tell the students to try to remain speaking for sixty seconds.

I find that this activity is pretty time efficient—taking only about ten minutes per week—and always has a freshening effect on my classroom cultures.

COMMON TEACHER HANG-UPS

I Have a Student Who Seems Completely Uninterested in Succeeding. What Should I Do?

Back in the 1980s, researcher Wlodkowski (1983) conducted a study that asked teachers to converse with target students for two straight minutes on a nonacademic topic, ten class days in a row. This "2x10" intervention, Wlodkowski found, was remarkably predictive of improved classroom dynamics going forward. And while I know of no peer-reviewed replication of Wlodkowski's results, there are hundreds of testimonials online of teachers who have used this strategy to great effect over the past thirty years.[53]

To me, Wlodkowski's 2x10 method is perfect for using with a student who seems especially resistant to defining success. To begin, take a class roster and select the student you are most concerned about. That phrase—"most concerned about"— deserves a bit more explanation. Here's how I select students for a 2x10 intervention:

- Is there someone in class who seems especially uninterested in thinking of success in any way? (This is our current scenario.)

- Is there someone in class who seems more prone than others to learning-disruptive behaviors?

- Is there someone in class who seems more prone than others to disengaging from a certain mode of work in class (e.g., reading independently, participating in group problem-solving conversations, elaborating during public speaking exercises)?

- Who in my class seems the most socially withdrawn from the rest of the group?

---

[53]If you're thinking that Wlodkowski's 2x10 sounds a lot like Strategy 1: Track Attempted MGCs, you're not crazy. However, 2x10 is different from Strategy 1 in two important ways: First, it takes place over the course of ten consecutive class periods; and second, the content of each of these ten conversations is personal, not academic.

Now obviously, questions like these are bound to lean toward my biases. Because of this, I like to keep track of who I do a 2x10 with over the course of a semester. This allows me to periodically review whom I've selected to see if my selections properly reflect the various diversities in my classroom.

Once I've selected a student, I take a blank index card, write the student's initials on it, and make a set of ten checkboxes with the next ten dates of instruction on it. As I complete each day's 2x10 with the student (often during an independent work segment of the lesson), I make notes of any nonacademic interest that the student alludes to (example below).

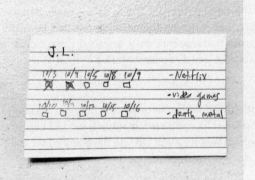

sample 2x10 index card tracker

I like to tape these onto my desk right next to my computer where I take attendance. Sometimes I have an index card for each of the class periods I teach.

During the first few days of a 2x10 intervention, I find the work to be very challenging. Target students tend to be uncomfortable speaking with a teacher at length—and trust me, two minutes is quite a length, at first! I approach those early conversations by saying things like this:

- "Hey Ruben, I was just thinking the other day that I don't really know much about you and I would love to. Nothing crazy—just, say, what do you like to do when you're not in

(Continued)

(Continued)

- "Carlei, I notice that you're always drawing in my class. I know, I know—sometimes I've gotten on your case for that. But I realized the other day that I've never asked you about how this interest came to you and how you got so good! Tell me about it."

Almost always I find that by the third or fourth day of a 2x10 sequence, these conversations become much more comfortable and natural.

- "Ruben, I looked up that show on Netflix that you mentioned, the documentary that you said is really sad. Holy cow—just watching the trailer made me sad! How did you come across that documentary, anyway? I don't often meet students who watch documentaries in their spare time."

- "Carlei, I made this doodle the other day during a meeting I was attending—just like you said, it actually kind of kept me focused on what I was hearing! Do you have any cool new drawings or doodles today?"

What's remarkable is that, by the end of the two weeks, you've invested only twenty minutes of total class time and almost always have arrived at a place unthinkable with that student only weeks before. Why does 2x10 work so well? I suspect that part of it is because students whom we're concerned about are not used to receiving consistent, nonthreatening attention like this from a teacher. They begin to look forward to the interactions and see us as someone who genuinely cares (rather than someone who is seeking to engineer a relationship for the sake of making their job easier).

Now of course it's up to you and me to make sure these attempts are as genuine as we can possibly make them. Don't overlook this important internal work.

I Have a Student Who Has Told Me That Their Guardian Doesn't Care About Their Success in School. What Can I Do?

For something like this, I think two things are important:

- First, even if your student feels that their guardian doesn't care about their success, you should not make the same assumption. We as educators can't assume anything about a student's home life or family situation except that students' guardians do care about their success just as much as their teachers.

- Second, try making a positive parent connection (via phone or e-mail) about something that you specifically appreciate about the student in question. Since this is such a low-Effort task, I've spoken with many teachers over the years who make positive parent contact a part of their daily routine.

Here's how a teacher from Baltimore describes this process:

> I like to do this via a quick phone call at the end of my work day. I keep a clipboard sheet just for this purpose, right next to my phone. Using the (not always perfect) data that I have for each student, I attempt the phone numbers on record. Whether I get a voicemail or a live person, I leave a simple message sharing something that I specifically appreciate about the parent or guardian's student.

In terms of the Five Key Beliefs, in these brief interactions that teacher is signalling to guardians that he genuinely cares about the student and is grateful to have the student in his class.

In my own attempts at this kind of strategy, this is what these positive parent phone calls can sound like.

(Continued)

(Continued)

EXAMPLES OF POSITIVE PARENT CONTACT

"Hi there, is this Roneisa's parent or guardian? This is Mr. Stuart—I teach Roneisa's third-hour world history class. Don't worry—I'm not calling for anything unpleasant! I actually just wanted to take sixty seconds and tell you how much I appreciate your young lady. She brings a bright smile to the room each day, and just this morning she asked a question in the middle of class that sparked some great follow-up discussion amongst her classmates. She really is a special young lady—and hey, I just wanted to let you know that I see that and I am grateful I get to teach her! If you ever need anything, just let me know, all right? Take care."

"Hello, is Jonathan's parent or guardian available? This is Mr. Stuart calling, Jonathan's world history teacher. I'm actually calling to quickly let you know that I so appreciate the thoughtful writing Jonathan does in my classroom. I was just looking over student warm-ups this afternoon during my prep period, and I couldn't help but note that Jonathan always seems to go the extra mile when he writes this. That is such an honorable thing to do—I really respect it!

"Anywho—I don't mean to take up more of your time, I just wanted you to know that I think Jonathan's great and am glad that I get to be his teacher. Thank you for being his parent guardian! As a parent myself, I know it's not easy. Take care."

Jason Schultz, a secondary educator at Divine Savior Academy in Doral, Florida, does something like this but digitally. Every day before he leaves work, he looks at his "Before I Leave" checklist. One of the items on that list is, "Send a parent/guardian e-mail." Jason peruses the document he keeps track of these e-mails on, selects a student he hasn't e-mailed yet this school year, and writes a quick paragraph or two very much in the spirit of the examples I shared above. When I was leading a workshop at Jason's school and he shared this strategy with me, he said he had lost count of the number of times he's heard back from a parent about how much these e-mails mean.

Both of these methods—phone or e-mail—take roughly five minutes per workday and result in about one contact attempt per student home per year. To me, this is a no-brainer transaction because you're significantly widening the reach of your care signalling—it's now not just to your students but also to their homes—and this inevitably leads to more discussion outside of your classroom about the fact that you are a good teacher that cares about each student. So, in that sense, it helps with Credibility.

But to bring it back to our hang-up, when dealing with students who are telling you that success in school is not something that their parent or guardian cares about, these positive touch points between the home and school make it more likely that school will be viewed as important at home.

Strategy 9: Unpack Outcomes, Good or Bad

In order to deepen their understanding of success and Effort, students need regular chances to reflect on what works and what doesn't. Most often, you can guide them in this all together as a whole class. Sometimes, however, certain kinds of individual unpacking sessions can be super powerful for learners.

What to Do

- Unpack outcomes as a whole class via methods such as
    - a post-unit individual reflection (pages 208–209),
    - a post-performance group reflection (pages 209–210), or
    - an exam wrapper (page 210).[54]
- Unpack outcomes individually via methods such as
    - the ten-minute meeting with a student who has experienced effortful failure (pages 211–213) or
    - an MGC series where you ask students about something they've succeeded in this year and what went into that (pages 214–215).

Key Pointer

This is a strategy whose power comes over time. Every time you attempt one of its methods, remind your students that you're doing this because their success *matters*—both to you as their teacher and to them as the folks who are living their lives.

[54]Thank you to Dave Steakley of the Lake Tahoe area for introducing me to exam wrappers.

How Strategy 9 Influences the Five Key Beliefs

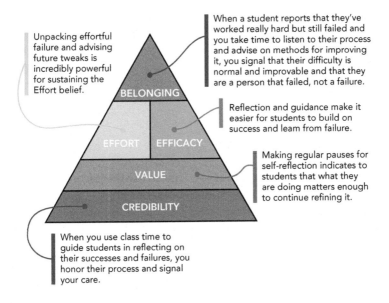

Unpacking effortful failure and advising future tweaks is incredibly powerful for sustaining the Effort belief.

When a student reports that they've worked really hard but still failed and you take time to listen to their process and advise on methods for improving it, you signal that their difficulty is normal and improvable and that they are a person that failed, not a failure.

Reflection and guidance make it easier for students to build on success and learn from failure.

Making regular pauses for self-reflection indicates to students that what they are doing matters enough to continue refining it.

When you use class time to guide students in reflecting on their successes and failures, you honor their process and signal your care.

WHY THIS STRATEGY

Strategies 7 and 8 make it all but inevitable that your students will put forth more Effort in your classroom—perhaps more than they ever have in school. This is just a natural by-product of creating a space in which effective learning is *explicitly taught, modeled, and reinforced*, and *genuine success is understood, valued, and pursued*.

Unfortunately, all the Effort in the world can't guarantee that your students will never fail. When they do, however, you have a powerful opportunity to impact them positively for the rest of their lives. In situations of what I call effortful failure—"Mr. Stuart, I studied for five hours before the test and I still failed"—students are primed for a learning breakthrough.

Strategy 9's prize move, then, is intervening in situations of effortful failure. But more broadly, it hinges on making post-Effort reflection a normal rhythm of your classroom. You don't just want students to put forth Effort—you want them to become increasingly thoughtful about the Effort that they have put forth and what results that Effort has resulted in. In doing this, you'll also make them more thoughtful about success as well. It's wins all around.

I'll share four methods that I use each year in my classroom. Two can be done with a whole room of students, and two seem to work best when done one-on-one. Remember that they are both skills, and as such practice will make you better at them so long as you yourself reflect on what works when you enact them and what doesn't.

Method 1: Unpack Outcomes as a Whole-Class Via Post-Unit Reflection.

On the first day after a unit finishes, I like to use the lesson warm-up as a chance for my students to reflect on the previous unit's work. Here are some examples of what this has looked like in my class.

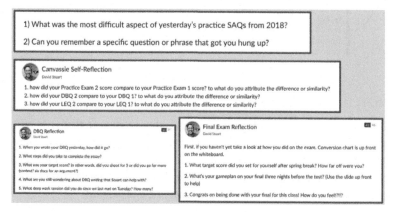

Sample Warm-Up Reflection Prompts from One of My Classes

Please note that I don't spend long amounts of time plotting these questions out. It's less premeditated and scientific than it is in-the-moment-before-class and instinctual. As I'm typing the questions, I'm asking myself, "How can I help my students to unpack how things went?"

After students complete their answers in writing, I may review their responses (via Canvas) or ask students to share what they've written with their partner. Here are some examples of the kinds of things students say:

- "I had a hard time breaking down the prompt. The wording was confusing to me. And so I muddled up my thesis."

- "My Unit 2 assessment score was worse than my Unit I assessment score, and at first I am not sure why. It is frustrating. But now that I think on it, I do see that I was pretty sleep-deprived for my Unit 2 test. This unit, I want to focus on getting better sleep each night."

- "When I was writing my essay, I began by reading the documents I was going to be citing from and grouping them into broad categories. I knew that these categories would probably become my body paragraphs."

Method 2: Unpack Outcomes as a Whole Class Via a Group Reflection.

If you want your students to reflect on something they've done as a whole class—for example, a whole class debate, let's say, or a read-aloud performance from *Romeo and Juliet*, or a lab experiment, or a game of flag football—a simple method is as follows:

1. Once the whole-class experience has ended, ask students to take sixty seconds to write down (or think about) something that the class did well and something that the class could improve upon next time.

2. After the brief thinking time period, ask students to share their strength and weakness responses with a partner.

3. Finally, have students share out to the whole class what they thought the class did well and what it could improve upon. I like to record these answers someplace that we can refer back to the next time we conduct this kind of exercise (e.g., a poster paper anchor chart).

This method is both quick and effective. Here are some examples of the kinds of things students say:

- "Often times in the discussion we got repetitive. We said the same things, over and over again. I think we could improve on that."

- "When we were preparing for the lab today, it seemed like there were too many people at the supply cabinet at a time.

Next time, maybe we could assign one person per group to access the cabinet so that it wouldn't feel so chaotic."

- "During the woodshop work time today, I noticed that a few of us wasted wood because we didn't measure twice before cutting. This is something that's tempting to take a shortcut on but that we ought to avoid in the future."

Method 3: Use an Exam Wrapper to Help Students Reflect on How They Prepared for a Test and How It Turned Out.

The American Psychological Association recommends that secondary and postsecondary students be given the opportunity to complete an "exam wrapper" (Lovett, 2013). There are two parts to this process: one that takes place before a major assessment and one that takes place after (i.e., it "wraps" around the test).

At least a few days prior to the exam, students are asked to reflect on

- what content they are and are not yet comfortable with,
- what grade they would expect to get if they had to take the test right now, and
- what they plan to do between now and exam time to improve their preparedness.

After the exam students complete additional reflective tasks, including

- tallying the cause of questions missed (e.g., misremembered, misunderstood, misread, etc);
- indicating specific preparation methods used prior to the exam (e.g., self-quizzing, partner-quizzing, spaced practice, etc.); and
- making an implementation intention for the next time the student prepares for an exam.

This simple process takes about thirty minutes during the first go with students but becomes more efficient as they get used to the process.

Scan this QR code to access the APA's handy, student-centered PDF for this process.

Method 4: When a Student Indicates That They've Worked Hard and Still Failed, Ask to Meet With Them for Ten Minutes as Soon as They're Able.

Few things are as demoralizing for a human being than working hard at something, feeling confident going into the thing they've worked hard at, and then failing miserably to reach their goals. Because of this, the method I'm about to describe is one of the few times that I recommend secondary teachers conduct one-on-one interventions with students. The reason I do so is because it works incredibly well and can make a big difference in the life of the learner.

Whenever a student reports this experience of "effortful failure" to me, I ask them if we can meet briefly either after school or during lunch sometime in the next couple days. To avoid making them anxious, I tell them simply that I care about what they've reported to me and I want to ask them more about what kind of Effort they put in and see if we can find a way to get better results for the Effort next time.

During the meeting, I do just what I've described:

- I begin by saying that I empathize with the pain of effortful failure, and I tell them that I want us to get to the bottom of what happened.

- I ask them to describe to me exactly what their Effort looked like; to help, I ask them questions like:

  o How long did you work?

  o How many work sessions did you work?

  o How distracting was the environment within which you worked?

- ○ What kinds of things did you do during your work sessions?

- ○ Did you ever become confused during your work sessions? If so, what did you do with that confusion?

- I then grab an index card and tell them I see just a few things they can try next time that will help them get better results. As I'm explaining my one, two, or three recommendations—no more than three, ever—I write them down as a bulleted list on an index card. (See chart below for common student hang-ups and the solutions I recommend.)

These are the most common ways that my ninth graders misapply Effort in the learning process.

COMMON STUDENT HANG-UP	RECOMMENDATION I GIVE THE STUDENT
The student multitasks while studying, which can look like switching between answering e-mails, checking text messages, reviewing flashcards, looking in the textbook, etc.	Do one thing at a time for each twenty-five-minute work session that you give to your studying. For example, during this session, review flashcards, and when you're done with the flashcards quiz yourself with your notes.
The student studies when exhausted and falls asleep.	Sleep begets learning—"If you have to pick between studying and sleep," I tell my students, "pick sleep." With that said, you often don't need to do this. If a student has a jammed evening schedule (e.g., sports, clubs, family responsibilities), I encourage them to set a regular time each week to come and work in my classroom before or after school or during lunch.
The student studies for long periods of time without brain breaks.	I teach my students to think of studying in terms of twenty-five-minute "deep work" sessions. No matter how big the study task, I tell them to break the work down into twenty-five-minute sessions. When

COMMON STUDENT HANG-UP	RECOMMENDATION I GIVE THE STUDENT
	the timer goes off, they should take a five-minute restorative break—something like a walk or a chat with family tends to work best.
The student "studies" by re-reading things or "looking over" their notes.	This is a classic pitfall for students because it makes them familiar with the source material—e.g., they start to really recognize what the textbook pages or their notes look like—yet they are unable to retrieve the concepts from their own mind. The best solution here is self-quizzing. I tell them to use their hand to cover up portions of the notes or the textbook and ask themselves, "What's under here? How does that relate to the previous concept or the next one?" Self-quizzing is one of those things I find the need to constantly practice with my secondary students; there seems to be a gravitational pull toward ineffective familiarization-based study methods.
The student studies in a needlessly distracting environment.	The most common example of this is when a student studies with their cell phone sitting next to them. This creates something that you could call the Phone-Nearby-While-You-Study Hamster Wheel Effect (scientific diagram below). The solution here is for the student to turn their phone off and place it just outside the door of the room they're working in. It's extreme, but the students crazy enough to try it each year consistently tell me how much it helps. And guess what? You can tell the student that if they're dying to read that text, they can go ahead and check the phone during their five-minute break.

The Phone-Nearby-While-You-Study Hamster Wheel Effect

Photo by Brooke Fournier. Hamster-wheel icon from iStock.com/Aleksei Gerasimenko.

Method 5: Complete an MGC Series (see Strategy 1) in Which You Ask Students to Describe Something They've Succeeded at in the Past.

The idea here is that, for an entire MGC series—that is, one full clip-board sheet (see page 55 for details)—you ask individual students to describe for you a time that they've succeeded in the past. When students have a hard time recalling a situation like this, I ask them things like, "What about in the realms of video games? Hobbies? What kinds of things do you do for fun but other folks find challenging?"

Once they share, ask a follow-up question or two that helps them unpack the success:

- What tactics did you use to succeed like that?
- What setbacks did you encounter on the path to that success? How did you overcome them?
- How did it feel when you first succeeded at that? Who did you tell?

As with the previous methods, this method gets students thinking and talking about what specific outcomes they are seeing and what specific actions of theirs cause these outcomes to come to pass.

All of these four methods will help you create a classroom context in which both Effort and success are contemplable, improvable, analyzable phenomena.

COMMON TEACHER HANG-UPS

This Student Says They Tried, but They Didn't.

Are you sure they didn't try? How do you know? If you don't have strong, evidence-based answers to those two questions, it's best to dissuade yourself from assumptions like this. They'll only embitter you.

If you indeed know that a student didn't try at something, however, the next thing is to examine the problem via the Five Key Beliefs.

- Credibility: Does the student believe you're good at your job? Do they believe that you care? Do they believe that you know what you're doing? If not, seek to remedy this problem via Strategies 1, 2, and 3. After all, when was the last time you felt motivated to try hard for a noncredible boss?

- Value: Does the student give any indication that they find this kind of work valuable? If not, seek to remedy this via Strategies 4, 5, and 6. Keep in mind, however, that these strategies are long-term plays. Value moves more slowly than we'd like, but it does move if we endure in signalling the Value of what we're doing.

- Effort and Efficacy: Does the student know what smart, effective Effort looks like? Have you gone out of your way, John Wooden style, to be explicit? If not, see Strategy 7. Does the student have a reasonable definition of success for your class? If not, see Strategy 8.

- Belonging: Does the student indicate that they believe they don't belong in your class or that they are uniquely bad at the work you're asking them to do? If so, see Strategy 10.

(Continued)

Effort & Efficacy

(Continued)

When students don't try, our conclusions must be wiser and more nuanced than, "Well, this student is just lazy." We must focus on what we control—our cultivation of the Five Key Beliefs—and refrain from making character-based assumptions about what a student is or is not.

I Have a Student Who Suffers From Severe Test Anxiety. What Can I Do to Help Them?

I'll always remember the lunch period when Grace came to me to unpack how she had been doing on tests. Before I could ask her anything, she shared a bit breathlessly how anxious she was becoming about tests in my class.

She had actually been doing all right on tests at the start of the year, but then at the end of our third unit, she had an outcome that, to her, was shockingly bad. By the time Unit 4's test came around, she was nervous the whole day of the test, and even while the test was happening she was noticing herself being worried about it. She ended up doing poorly again on that test. And now here she was, talking to me about test anxiety.

She reminded me a lot of me during the first seven or so years of my speaking career. During those days, whenever I would see a speaking engagement coming up on the calendar—a PD or a keynote for teachers, typically—I would start feeling a fluttery-queasy kind of nervousness. This would continue all the way up to the moment that I was introduced at the event. I bet I experienced this hundreds of times.

In other words, I could relate to Grace's struggle. *And* I could even recall times when the nervousness became debilitating—exactly like Grace was experiencing it. So I shared with Grace a simple trick: When you're feeling nervous before a test, literally say out loud to yourself (or write in all caps at the top of the test), "I am excited." This sounds ridiculous, but it's actually vetted in the research (Brooks, 2014). But since it sounds ridiculous, I wanted to share with Grace how it works.

The gist is this: When you're nervous, that's a heightened state of psychological arousal, and heightened states of psychological arousal are tough to shoehorn down into calmness. This is why the most common advice given to folks who are nervous before a test or a performance—"Oh, don't worry! You've got this. It's going to be fine. *Relax.*"—is actually super unhelpful. It's really hard to simply will yourself from a high state of arousal to a low one. So instead, when you feel those nerves kicking in, you tell yourself that you're excited: "I'm not nervous—I'm excited."

"So Grace," I said, "Think of it like this: Tell yourself, 'I'm *jacked*. I've been preparing for this test *all month*. I get to see some novel test questions today. I get to see where I'm at as a learner. Sweet. Awesome. *Yes.*'"

It sounds super dumb, actually. But the crazy thing is, Grace found that it worked. On her final exam that year, Grace did the "I'm excited" self-talk and had her best ever performance on the test.

What's even more important to me is that, as she was taking the test, I caught her smiling.

Effort & Efficacy

Belonging

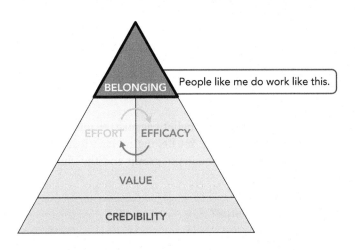

BELONGING — People like me do work like this.

EFFORT ⟳ EFFICACY

VALUE

CREDIBILITY

WHAT **BELONGING** SOUNDS LIKE	WHAT **ANTI-BELONGING** SOUNDS LIKE
People like me read.	None of my friends read because we're just not into that sort of thing.
I'm a science kid.	I don't get science.
I'm not a poser in here; these are my people, and I'm theirs.	People who care about school are posers or try-hards. I'm not like them.
It's not weird that I'm writing right now because people like me write.	I'm not a writer.
I'm shy, but I still stand up for pop-up debates because plenty of people in our class are shy, and we challenge ourselves through public speaking.	I'm too shy to participate.
My contributions and abilities are valued by this community.	People think I don't have what it takes to be in here.
The things I struggle with are normal for people in this community.	I'm the only one having a hard time in here.

*The more accepted, cared for, safe, and connected kids feel
in their schools, the better their lives will be according to just
about any measure.*

—EDUCATOR-AUTHOR JESSICA LAHEY

Our final belief—the capstone of our Five Key Beliefs pyramid—is
Belonging. It largely comes down to two sorts of questions in the
hearts of our students:

I. Who am I? What is my identity? What makes me, me?

2. Does who I am fit here—with these people, studying this
   discipline, doing this kind of work?

Years ago, I called this the Identity belief because the question "Who
am I?" is so central to its nature. Yet Belonging isn't just about the
individual—it's just as much about the group and the context. It's
not just "Who am I?" It's:

- "Who am I, *in this context*?"
- "Who am I, *with these people*?"
- "What do the things that happen to me in this classroom
  mean?"
- "How do *I* fit *here*?"

Whenever I think about Belonging, I typically think of three stories.
Two of them involve my children and one involves my students. The
first story is funny; the second and third are magic.

In the first story, my daughter Laura and her siblings and I were
doing post-dinner chores. It was a Monday evening, and so the kids'
chores had rotated since the previous week.

"What are you on this week, Laura?" I asked.

"Hmm, let me check." A pause. "Oh no!"

"What!?"

"Vacuuming!? I wasn't born to vacuum, Dad!! I am *not* a vacuum person."

Laura perfectly (and humorously) demonstrated the important power of the Belonging belief: It's hard being motivated to do work that does not fit with your identity.

In the second story, we head to the backyard swimming pool of Ms. Rita, where she taught a legendary survival swim school for children for over thirty years. Most students began the week of five one-hour lessons terrified of swimming, unwilling even to put their heads under water; by the end, over 90 percent of Ms. Rita's students were capable swimmers growing in their confidence. All of our four children were fortunate to have Ms. Rita as a teacher.

After our children completed the swim school, strangers would often ask us at pools and lakes how we got our children to swim with such confidence and joy. The truth is, it was about five hours of very basic, simple, and effective instruction and practice. This transition from fear to empowerment led to a shift in how our children thought of themselves in relation to water. In other words, it was a shift in Belonging. All of our children shifted from saying, "I hate going in the water," into affirming, "I'm a swimmer." A teacher did that.

And for the third story, we head to a nondescript classroom in rural-suburban western Michigan: my own.

Rebecca's story isn't uncommon. At the start of the school year, Rebecca was worried sick during our first pop-up debate. "I felt like I was going to throw up" were the words Rebecca used when I asked her about it. But as the year progressed, I worked to normalize (Strategy 10) public speaking anxiety and Woodenize (Strategy 7) the living daylights out of all aspects of pop-up debate.[55] And as time went on, some remarkable shifts began to happen in Rebecca's heart:

- She grew in confidence.
- She started looking forward to pop-up debates.

Belonging

[55]For a full treatment of pop-up debate, see Chapters 4 and 7 of my book *These 6 Things*.

- She began standing up in the debates without being called upon.

- She began using her extra, nonmandatory speech opportunities.

- She started to think that her future may be one in which public speaking was a central part.[56]

In all of these stories, we see the powerful role that Belonging plays in motivation—in things as minor as vacuuming to those as consequential and scary as swimming or public speaking.[57]

Now let's look at some key understandings for the Belonging belief.

Key Understanding 1: Belonging Signals Are Ambiguous.

If I walk up to you and have a neutral expression, what does that signal to you? Does it mean that I respect you? That I'm glad to see you? That I'm annoyed by you? That I find you repulsive? Or, what if I walk up to you and smile? Does it mean that I respect you? Is the smile genuine or fake? Am I glad to see you, or am I trying to hide that I'm annoyed by you?

This is the trouble with signals in social contexts: They are ambiguous. They require interpretation. And in contexts as socially complex as schools, wow—what an overwhelming array of ambiguous signals all of us will find ourselves confronted by.

So, what the Belonging belief does is create a powerful lens through which to interpret ambiguous social signals—it turns them into motivators; it makes them safe. Anti-Belonging, on the other hand, does the opposite—it interprets ambiguous signals as signs of threat.

---

[56]In terms of the Rainbow of Why, this latter transformation was an opening of purpose inside of Rebecca's heart.

[57]Stories of Belonging happen in schools around the world, every day. Recently I met an art teacher in the Phoenix area named Carlos, and he told me the story of a student he taught who was very much into playing football. At the start of the semester, this student was quite vocal with Carlos about how he wasn't much of an artist. But then the student came into class one day to share with Carlos what he had noticed about the shading on a mural that had just been completed in his neighborhood. "Well," Carlos said to the student, "you sound an awful lot like an artist when you talk like that." The student grinned.

Belonging

AMBIGUOUS SIGNAL	BELONGING INTERPRETATION	ANTI-BELONGING INTERPRETATION
Mr. Stuart is looking neutrally at me.	He respects me. He takes me seriously.	He's annoyed by me. He doesn't like me.
Mr. Stuart is smiling at me.	He likes me. He's glad I'm here.	He thinks I'm a joke. He's faking to try to make me feel better.
Mr. Stuart just gave a confusing mini-lecture and when he asked, "What questions might you all have?" no one raised their hand.	I'm sure I'm not the only one who is confused after that. I'm going to raise my hand and voice what a lot of us are probably thinking.	I must be the idiot in the room. Everyone else gets it, but I don't.
We just ran the mile in phys ed, and I got twelfth place.	It's because we have different bodies and different physical histories. This is where I'm at right now in my fitness journey. It's not a good thing or a bad thing—it just is what it is.	I hate phys ed. I'm too slow to fit in here. Everyone must be laughing at me behind my back.
The teacher called on the person next to me when my hand was raised too.	It happens! No big deal. I'm loved and valued here.	The teacher must not like me. The teacher must think I'm dumb.

Key Understanding 2: The Way Students Interpret Signals of Belonging Becomes Recursive if Left Untreated.

Because Belonging signals are ambiguous, much of a student's sense of Belonging lies in how they interpret those signals. If the interpretations are helpful—see the green column above—then the students' sense of Belonging will be strengthened over time in a manner akin to the fly-wheel effect that we saw on page 170 with Effort and Efficacy.

But if the interpretations are not helpful—see the red column above—then the student's sense of Belonging will diminish over time in something that we could rightly call a doom loop. Here it will be easiest for me to explain using a graphic.

The ANTI-Belonging Loop

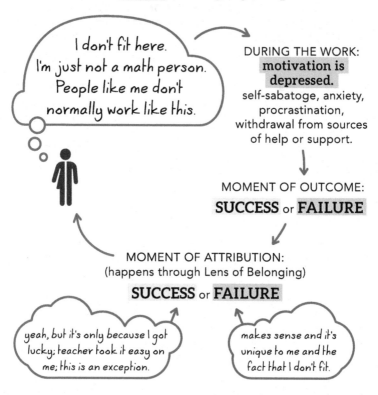

In the upper-left corner we have a student in, let's say, a mathematics class. The student has just begun his tenth-grade year with Mr. Modisher, and because of a multitude of experiences and factors that Mr. Modisher could not control, this student enters the class believing things like we see in the thought bubble above.

Over the course of the first week, Mr. Modisher does his best to use the strategies outlined in this book, but our focal student is one that has struggled with Belonging in mathematics for many years. This will not be an overnight change for the student. And so, during those early math lessons and assignments that Mr. Modisher provides the student with, the first by-product of anti-Belonging rears its head: The student has a hard time being motivated to try to try to learn. This demotivation comes from things such as the following:

- The Hamster Wheel effect—the student is so concerned about not fitting in here that he or she is hyperaware of how folks nearby may be perceiving him.

Belonging

- Self-sabotage—to protect himself, the student may put forth as little Effort as possible; after all, this way he doesn't need to face the disappointment of effortful failure.

- Procrastination—the student could find it difficult to attend to Mr. Modisher's lessons or homework until the very last minute—after all, no one wants to face the feeling of anxiety that a high schooler experiences when they don't fit in.

- Isolation—when Mr. Modisher circulates to confer with individual students, our focal student may bluff his way past Mr. Modisher's offers of guidance, saying he doesn't need help.

Eventually, the first formative assessment results start to come back. The student sees that he's getting questions wrong—lots of them. Or, perhaps the first unit of the year is quite remedial—perhaps the student surprises himself by doing well. This is where anti-Belonging bears its second unpleasant fruit: the moment of attribution. How is the student likely to interpret the outcomes of this first week of class? Because our student has a heavily entrenched anti-Belonging belief—and because of the ambiguity of Belonging signals—he is likely to interpret either success or failure in the same way—proof that he doesn't belong.

If he fails—the more likely outcome due to the demotivation that we saw in the "during the work" phase of the loop—then he will likely interpret the failure as further proof that he doesn't fit. It will reinforce his belief. But if he succeeds—very possible, given Mr. Modisher's skillful scaffolding during this initial week—he's likely to brush it off. He might think that Mr. Modisher was just being nice to the students, or he was making it too easy. Or perhaps our focal student was just lucky. And so the cycle continues.

Thankfully, you and I already have tools for remedying situations like this over the course of a semester. In fact, every single one of our strategies so far ministers to students who are caught in hard spots like our focal student:

- Strategy 1—Track Attempted MGCs—helps Mr. Modisher build a strong working relationship with the student; as time progresses, the student will grow in his perception that Mr. Modisher genuinely cares about his academic progress, and this will help the student to take advantage of Mr. Modisher's offers for help.

- Strategy 2—Improve at One Thing—has allowed Mr. Modisher to become an effective teacher during his career; as a result, Mr. Modisher is accustomed to working with tenth-grade students who are underprepared for tenth-grade mathematics and he has strategies that he's developed over time for helping them to catch up.

- Strategy 3—Gentle Urgency—means Mr. Modisher has more minutes to use for helping students like our focal student to make gains and catch up; this also communicates to the student over time that math might be more valuable than he previously perceived.

- Strategy 4—An Apologist, Winsome and Sure—has Mr. Modisher regularly commenting, in ways that line up with his personality, on how good and useful and even beautiful mathematics is; our focal student hasn't seen this before and is intrigued by it.

- Strategy 5—Feast of Knowledge—allows Mr. Modisher to sprinkle in stories from teaching his own children basic mathematics as they were growing up; this lets Mr. Modisher teach his tenth graders tricks for mastering basic math facts under the guise of sharing something he did with his children rather than as a bald-faced attempt to help his students fill in missing pieces;

- Strategy 6—Valued Within—means Mr. Modisher is regularly asking his students to explain for themselves what the Value of mathematics is; he has them answer the "When will I ever use this?" questions and celebrates novel answers to such questions with his students.

- Strategy 7—Woodenize All of It—is so powerful for our focal student because Mr. Modisher takes the time to teach every kid in the class how to do really basic things that the student thought only he didn't know. For example, Mr. Modisher teachers the basics of using a calculator, how to avoid common mistakes with multiplication, and other general things that our focal student assumed no one else still needed to learn.

- Strategy 8—Define Success: Wisely, Early, and Often—helps our student to gain a vision for this mathematics class that he's never had before; slowly, he's sensing that success in math, just like success in life, is about steady growth over time and about learning from setbacks.

- Strategy 9—Unpack Outcomes, Good or Bad—helps our student to see that everyone in class reflects on how things go in each unit; it's not just something non-math-inclined kids do. He starts to overhear the things other students are saying and begins to realize that almost everyone has at least some struggles during the growth journey of mathematics.

Key Understanding 3: Belonging Is Especially Challenging for Underrepresented Students Because of Two Related but Separate Phenomena: Imposter Syndrome and Stereotype Threat.

Imposter syndrome, first named by Clance and Imes (1978), is the feeling students have when they are convinced that they don't belong and are in fact acting fraudulently when engaging in a given academic pursuit. This could happen to a student in an honors mathematics class who does not believe that they ought to be in the class because no one else from their social group is there. Imposter syndrome can lead students to behave in various ways that further undermine their sense of Belonging.[58]

Stereotype threat is related but different. Coined by Steele and Aronson (1995), this phenomena happens when a student is concerned about confirming negative stereotypes that may be held about their group. In their original research, Steele and Aronson demonstrated that Black students performed more poorly than white peers when made aware of negative stereotypes associated with their racial group and that this gap in performance diminished when researchers took steps to alleviate the phenomena.

---

[58]In 1978, Clance and Imes observed the following "four different types of behaviors performed by women with imposter syndrome that perpetuate the phenomenon. The first behavior is engaging in diligence, which refers to women working hard to prevent others from discovering their status as an imposter. The second behavior is engaging in intellectual inauthenticity, which refers to women choosing to conceal their true ideas and opinions, and only voicing ideas and opinions they believe will be well received by their audience. The third behavior is engaging in charm, which refers to women seeking to gain the approval of their superiors by being well liked and perceived as intellectually special. The fourth and final behavior is avoiding displays of confidence, which refers to women being cognizant of society's rejection of successful women and consciously exhibiting themselves as timid" (Edwards, 2019).

Both imposter syndrome—the feeling that one does not belong—and stereotype threat—the feeling that one must prove that they *do* belong[59]—amount to similar experiences for the learner: anxiousness about fitting in, hypervigilance to signals of Belonging or anti-Belonging, and an unpleasant hamster wheel in the mind and heart.

Thankfully, these experiences can be improved for our students. Let's look at one quick method in the research for doing this, and then in Strategy 10: Normalize Struggle we'll dive into another.

Key Understanding 4: Belonging Can Be Influenced Positively via a Simple, Infrequent "Values Affirmation" Exercise.

Here's all that you do: Give your students fifteen to twenty minutes to write about two or three things that they personally value. To help get them thinking, it's often helpful to give them a list—I like to do this on a screen up front—of potential values to pick from.

INSTRUCTIONS: **Pick 2-3 things that you value and write a few sentences about each of them.** Why are these thing important to you? How do they make you feel?

- sports
- art
- reading
- movies
- gaming
- humor
- hobbies
- creativity
- discovering new things
- inventing things
- making a difference in the world
- being independent
- kindness
- enjoying today

- enjoying today
- living in the moment
- your friends
- your family
- your race
- your ancestry
- your community
- music
- doing the right thing
- nature
- the environment
- success in your career
- other:

_____

Belonging

---

[59]Researcher Edwards's (2019) paper on these phenomena was the first I read that arrived at this simple encapsulation of the two phenomena.

That's it. There's no need to discuss or share or anything else.

This remarkably simple exercise has been demonstrated in the research to have profound effects on Belonging. For example, in one study (Pyne & Borman, 2020) of two thousand middle school students across eleven racially diverse middle schools, students did this activity twice in the school year, once at the start and once during spring testing season. In the months after the intervention, "The black-white suspension and office referral gaps were cut by two-thirds, with an even more positive impact on black students with prior infractions" (Marshall, 2022). In other studies (e.g., Cohen et al., 2006, 2009; Miyake et al., 2010), students in stereotype-threatened groups who underwent this intervention earned higher grades over time.

As with all interventions like this, it is far from a silver bullet. But, given the simplicity of the task and the wonderful things you can learn about your students,[60] it's a total no-brainer to incorporate this kind of thing into every secondary school in the world.

---

[60]I'll never forget when Levi shared in his values affirmation write-up at the start of the year how much he valued riding his four-wheeler through open fields near his house. Before I read that, I had sensed in Levi a strong degree of anti-Belonging; he had written often in the early days of school about how he didn't like school at all. But reading his poetic description of riding on the quad changed how I viewed Levi ever after. I found it easier to genuinely appreciate his presence in class, and this genuine appreciation was likely palpable to Levi during at least some of my MGC attempts (Strategy 1) for the rest of the school year.

Belonging

Strategy 10: Normalize Struggle

When students aren't sure that they belong in your class as they're doing the work of learning you're asking them to do, then as soon as struggle comes they're likely to interpret it as a signal that yells, "This is struggle unique to *you*; *you* don't belong!" This creates a hamster wheel effect on their mind, making them hyperalert to any other signals from your classroom that they don't fit. And because Belonging signals can be so ambiguous, the hamster wheel is more than just a little thing; it biases student hearts to interpret ambiguous signals as more of the "*You* don't belong" variety.

So here's a strong fix: Create an environment in which struggle is both normal and productive.

What to Do

- Make difficulty normal—that is, something that's not unique to the student how is struggling. Do this via moves such as
  - whole-class polling after something difficult or
  - asking students to explain difficulty to younger students using a "student-as-expert" prompt.
- Make critical feedback normal with Greg Cohen's "magic feedback" method. Tell students, in ways they can hear, that you're giving them honest feedback because you have high expectations and you know they can meet them.
- Make difficulty desirable—something they literally can't succeed without. Do this via moves such as
  - sharing stories of folks who link struggle to success (e.g., Josh Cooper's "Motivation Monday" videos) or
  - create a "Do hard things" ethos in your classroom.

Key Pointer

- You're trying to make difficulty normal. This signals against tendencies in our students' hearts toward believing anti-Belonging things like, "This math work is hard for me and *only* me. Other folks don't struggle like I do; I don't fit in here."

How Strategy 10 Influences the Five Key Beliefs

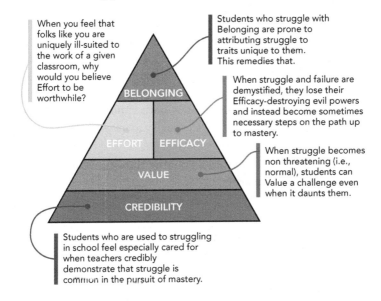

When you feel that folks like you are uniquely ill-suited to the work of a given classroom, why would you believe Effort to be worthwhile?

Students who struggle with Belonging are prone to attributing struggle to traits unique to them. This remedies that.

When struggle and failure are demystified, they lose their Efficacy-destroying evil powers and instead become sometimes necessary steps on the path up to mastery.

When struggle becomes non threatening (i.e., normal), students can Value a challenge even when it daunts them.

Students who are used to struggling in school feel especially cared for when teachers credibly demonstrate that struggle is common in the pursuit of mastery.

BELONGING

EFFORT EFFICACY

VALUE

CREDIBILITY

When we're not sure that we belong in a class, we get this hamster wheel effect going in our mind. This is what it looks like.

When a student struggles with Belonging, they become what social psychologists describe as hypervigilant. Basically, a part of their cognition is constantly spent monitoring the environment for signals that they might not fit in the context they're in. Given that students and teachers have limited bandwidth for focus already, this hypervigilant hamster wheel is harmful to learning.

Remember, too, that this hamster wheel is *painful*. It's unpleasant to always wonder if you belong, always scanning an environment for signals that you do or don't fit. And that, dear colleague, is what I call a double whammy: a student is both experiencing pain *and* experiencing diminished cognitive capacity to invest in gains.

Without a doubt, then, the Anti-Belonging Hamster Wheel Effect is something we'd like to disrupt.

Strategy 10 is aimed at just that: disrupting the hamster wheel by resolving the ambiguity of struggle. Instead of allowing struggle to be ambiguous, we seek to make it *ubiquitous*. We want classroom cultures where the struggle is normal as much as it's real. We're after places of learning where all of us seek the good feeling of doing hard things.

First, we want our students to see that all good learners struggle. To not experience any struggle at all means that you're either not trying or not setting your sights on worthy enough goals. I often make this claim to my students.

It reminds me of when, early on in our parenting years, Crystal and I were just coming to terms with the fact that there was lots we didn't know about raising a child. When speaking with more experienced parents or seeing families further along than ours, we would receive an ambiguous signal: Here is a couple that doesn't seem to struggle with the same things we do as parents; here is a family that does not seem to have our issues.

The insidiousness of the anti-Belonging hamster wheel is quick to take over in these kinds of uncertain situations. "Shoot!" our hearts intuit, "I don't fit here! I'm exceptionally bad! There's something about me that's not enough."

What helped most in situations like this was actually when the folks we were secretly admiring would say something like, "Oh my goodness, we had such a hard time with our daughter today," or "Wow, your children are so great, David and Crystal! We had no idea what we were doing back then." It messaged to us that, despite the isolation we felt, the struggle of parenting was not unique to us; it was common to folks who had gone before us. Folks who seemed to have it all together, didn't. And so we began to have more internal power to bring to bear on our parenting struggles because we could put to rest the idea that each struggle was unique to us. In other words, we started to feel that we *belonged* as parents.

We want this same sort of effect for each of our students. We want them to know that there are no achievers who do not struggle; there is no growth without the occasional setback. And when difficulty comes, it can be unpacked (Strategy 9), processed, and overcome.

HOW TO GAIN PROFICIENCY WITH STRATEGY 10

In order to achieve this kind of classroom environment, there are some very practical things that we can do. I'll present these methods in order, from the simplest to the most involved.

Method 1: Use the Whole-Class Poll of "Who Felt at Least 1 Percent Challenged?" After Completing Something Difficult.

After a significant classroom challenge—in my room, that's often our first pop-up debate of the school year or our first test—I like to normalize struggle by asking my students a simple prompt: "If you felt at least 1 percent nervous during the preceding activity, please raise your hand."

Every single time that I have done this after a whole-class speaking event like a pop-up debate, upwards of 70 percent of my students have raised their hands. This is a powerful moment for the Belonging belief, and I cement it with a remark such as, "Now class, look around you. Look at all the hands in the air. I want you to remember this. Anxiety is often a deceitful thing—it makes you think that it's only *you* who feels nervous. But look—look around you! It's not just you. When it comes to speaking in front of peers, it's most folks."

Here I begin to smile.

"It's those folks without their hands up that are the weirdos."

And with a wink and a grin, I've sent a quick but powerful signal: Struggle is normal in the high-challenge realm of public speaking.

You can do something similar after other activities, such as an assessment, a presentation, or a performance task.

The keys to success with this method include the following:

- Because your students (like mine) are broadly dispersed along a skill spectrum, make the initial challenge something that is inherently self-differentiating in its difficulty (e.g., a public speaking exercise or difficult pre-test). You want a majority of folks to be able to raise their hand afterwards saying, "Yes, that was difficult." And then you want to remind them that despite that difficulty, they came out on top (e.g., they participated despite public speaking anxiety or they previewed class content and the kinds of things they'd be learning this semester—despite not knowing everything, they learned).

- Provide adequate pre-experience practice and/or scaffolds so that all students can experience a modicum of success. In my case. for the first pop-up debate of the school year, this means that all of my students have participated in Think-Pair-Share on a daily basis and that I've called upon all of them to share to the whole class (during the share portion of Think-Pair-Share) at least once per week for three weeks prior to our first pop-up debate.

- Be sure to define what the bare minimum of success looks like for the activity. In my first pop-up debates, I tell students that success is simply standing up and participating at least once during the debate.

- Remind students after this experience of what they learned about the normality of challenge. I can't stress this enough; you must reinforce for your students how to helpfully interpret this signal. They need this signal reinforced so that they can attribute subsequent struggles to something that is

Belonging

normal for students rather than to something that is uniquely deficient in them.

Method 2: Ask Students to Explain Difficulty to Future Students.

This is what I call "student as expert." It's a brilliant move that comes from the wise intervention strand of the social psychology research, spearheaded in part by folks like Stanford's Greg Cohen and Greg Walton—two of the leading names in the work on cultivating the Belonging belief in educational settings.

Let's look at how this works.

First, expose students to a few testimonials from students who have come before them. These can be direct quotes from previous students, or video testimonials, or your own anecdotal recollections.

In the testimonials, try to hit the following notes:

- "At first, I struggled with _____ and thought it was something unique to me." (That last part is the key. Students need to hear from other students that they too thought they didn't belong.)

- "Then, I realized _____ was a normal struggle. I realized this when _____ happened to me or when _____ said _____ to me." (Here you want to make sure the student describes the moment that they realized it wasn't just them.)

- "Once I realized that this was a normal struggle, I started [insert adaptive behavior] and began to see progress and enjoyability in my growth." (Adaptive behaviors can include seeking help, attending study halls, or working more closely with friends.)

Then, ask students to explain to subsequent students why these stories make sense. In other words, enlist your current students as *experts* in helping subsequent students as *novices* navigate the

Belonging

ambiguity of struggle signals and interpret them as normal rather than as unique to them.

In the research, this powerful student-as-expert methodology is referred to as *attributional retraining*. It exposes students to

- folks just a bit older than them who are likely to sound much more believable than an "old person" (i.e., me) and
- the chance to position themselves as experts and interpret their own experience with the struggle toward mastery as something that is normal rather than aberrant.

The way I see it, attributional retraining is worth our time for a few reasons:

- The earliest step is where most of the labor is at, as collecting testimonials takes time and intentionality on the part of the teacher, team, or school. But what's brilliant here is that, once acquired, the testimonials from older students can be used again and again. Note that the testimonials have a certain pattern:
  - "I once struggled in school and assumed it was a struggle unique to me."
  - "Then something happened and I realized it wasn't just me."
  - "So then I started to reach out for assistance and was gladly given it."
- The last part of the method places a student in the position of expert. Rather than receiving advice, they are responsible for giving it. This is a remarkably powerful way to shape belief; it is not, "Let me tell you why you belong," but instead, "You tell me why you belong."
- Experts aren't just good for themselves, are they? They're good for *others*, too—thereby enacting the Value power of prosocial purpose that we looked at on page 111.

Let's look at what this might look like in, say, a physical education class. Once students are dressed and completing their stretching routine, the teacher shows a three-minute videotaped interview of a student who previously took the class. This student shares the following:

- They once thought phys ed wasn't for folks like them because they couldn't run that well.

- They came to discover that it was normal for phys ed students to experience this sense of anti-Belonging when their teacher told a story about a time in the teacher's life that they were out of shape and had to retrain themselves to run a mile.

- The student had a breakthrough by focusing on what they could control in the phys ed space, and they realized that physical fitness is all about taking risks[61] as an individual instead of comparing themselves to others.

Method 3: When You Give Students Critical Feedback, State That You're Giving It to Them Because You Have High Expectations That You Know They Can Meet.

Some years ago, Stanford's Geoffrey Cohen led a team of researchers to see if a certain way of framing critical feedback from teacher to student might improve student experiences in school. The intervention worked so well that Coyle (2018) later popularized it as "magic feedback." The tweak was remarkable—"magic," in Coyle's words—in at least two ways: first, it was simple, and second, it was effective.

In the study, college students in the experimental condition were told, "I'm giving you this feedback because I have high expectations and I know you can meet them," whereas students in the control condition were simply given the critical feedback without the magical line. Those who received the magical line were more likely to make revisions to their essays and indicate that they trusted their teachers (Yeager et al., 2014).

Now obviously, the feedback wasn't a magic spell. My point in sharing it is not that you'll photocopy a bunch of little lines like this and paste them into your Google Classroom response templates. Rather, it's

---

[61]Props to the secondary physical education team in New Buffalo, Michigan, for this language affirming phys ed is all about taking risks. I love it.

that you'll internalize this idea that your students need to hear *both* that you have high expectations for your students and that you know *this particular student* can reach those expectations.

Method 4: Make Difficulty Desirable; Make It *Odd* and *Unseemly* to Not Seek Some Measure of Challenge in a Given Class.

The best way that I've found for doing this is to frame secondary education as a worthy challenge for any youngster. I want to make "doing hard things" an ideal for my students, not a chore. I do this via the following:

- Hanging a sign above my whiteboard that reads "Do hard things." I periodically explain what I mean with this sign via micro-sermons (see Strategy 4 on page 123).

- Celebrating when a student overcomes challenge. I want to highlight the moment in their mind as a beautiful, even transcendental experience.

- Challenging common notions that my students or the broader culture hold regarding low expectations or comparing oneself to an arbitrary measure.

Our colleague Josh Cooper who teaches economics does this a bit differently using a program he's developed called "Motivation Mondays." He likes to use this program in his general econ classes—the ones where students are there because the state requires it.

Each Monday, Mr. Cooper kicks class off after the warm-up with a brief video from former U.S. Navy SEAL Jocko Willink. The video is titled "This Is Gonna Suck," and in it Jocko, in memorable style, elaborates on the idea that good things are often hard. "This advice," Mr. Cooper says to his students, "is simple but not easy—just like a lot of others keys to success in life.

The next week Mr. Cooper shares a video titled "Look for Work," in which Jocko describes how he expects his SEAL team members to be always looking to improve. After sharing this video, Mr. Cooper will use this language with his students when they finish a task early.

A few weeks later, Mr. Cooper shares a Jocko video titled "Bust That Door," in which the main idea is that when you are confronted with a hard task, the most difficult but best thing is to get started. Mr. Cooper likes to connect this to his students' propensity for procrastination. "Procrastination seems goods in the moment," he says, "but it typically doesn't help you." And so on he goes, using Jocko's brief videos from Instagram to give his students a dose of perspective on struggle from a former SEAL.

Here's why it works:

- Mr. Cooper's prep for this is minimal. He keeps a running list in his e-mail inbox of videos that could work with his students.

- His source (Jocko) is novel to most students (this helps with Value) and inherently credible.

- He is dropping in these moments occasionally over time rather than relying on big chunks of class time.

COMMON TEACHER HANG-UPS

Some of My Students Struggle Much More Than Their Peers and They Are Very Self-Conscious of This.

This hang-up reminds me of a student I taught not that long ago—let's call her Lindsay.

Lindsay was warm and beaming during the first week of school. She was outgoing and positive; I can still remember the "Be the best at being kind" T-shirt that she wore during that first week. She really was the best at being kind.

Over that first semester, however, I saw Lindsay's affect slowly drain of its winsome energy. That bright spirit from the first week seemed to exactly track with her performance in the class: As the units came and went, her declining results on formative and summative assessments deeply disappointed her. What was worse, though, is that I could sense that Lindsay was starting to believe

(Continued)

Belonging

that she had no business being in this class with her peers. She was convinced that her performance was uniquely bad—when she and her friends would gather when class ended, I could feel her pain each time someone asked, "How'd you do on the assessment?" She knew she'd have the worst score in the group.

It was a classic case of anti-Belonging taking root in the heart of a young person. And for months and months, I had a hard time dislodging it, *despite* my efforts with all the strategies in this book. It was the kind of thing I see each year in my classroom practice. Five Key Beliefs work is gardening, not button-pushing. You control only so much. Sometimes the pains you seek to mend are stubbornly resilient.

The moment of change came at the start of second semester. During an MGC attempt in the hallway (Strategy 1), I conversed with Lindsay about how she felt her first semester had gone. Her eyes went downcast instantly.

"Lindsay," I said. "Can I ask you a different question? Do you ever compare yourself to the other students in class?"

She looked right up at me, startled.

"Yes."

"All right. Wow—that was honesty right there, and I want to tell you that I appreciate that. That's real stuff. Gosh, do you have courage. Thank you."

"Okay." Smile.

"Lindsay, what if we did this: What if the whole goal this semester was for Lindsay in three months to be someone stronger and smarter and more capable than Lindsay today? In other words, what if you and I made a pact that the only person you needed to compare yourself to for the next three months was you? What if you and I said, 'That's what success is this semester for Lindsay—self-improvement?'"

She nodded.

"Could we do that?"

She nodded again.

"All right—let's do that. And throughout that whole process, is it all right if I remind you sometimes when we're in one-on-one moments like this that you absolutely belong in *this* class with *this* group of people? Would that be all right?"

She nodded a third time.

That was all there was to the interaction, but it really made a difference. I saw a loosening in Lindsay's affect begin that day, a slow return to the bright spirit from the first week of the school year.

During the last week of school, Lindsay's class and I were out on a walk after our final exam was completed when Lindsay surprised us all by having her mom bring popsicles out to us on the walking trail. There she was, beaming amongst all her classmates—all of whom had struggled that year, none of whom had struggled in the exact same way.

Conclusion: Healers of Souls

During the final months of writing this book, I received an incoming call from a number I didn't know. It had a Baltimore area code.

"Hello?" I said.

"Mr. Stuart? This is Brian."

It was Brian Lawrence—a student I taught as a seventh grader. At the time he was calling me, he was twenty-seven years old.

We small-talked for a few minutes, and then Brian said, "Mr. Stuart, you're the reason I started to love reading."

Now, I love Brian's generosity in saying that. I receive his kind and good words as the treasure chests they are. What a priceless gift, to have a human being say thank you to their teacher. But I know that there are many reasons Brian came to love reading, and mastery and its delightful benefits come to those who do work with care. Actions *he* took, in other words, were the primary reason that he came to love reading. True, some of those actions were actions I required as his teacher; some of those heart shifts were aided by things that I did, all those years ago, that unbeknownst to me were cultivating the Five Key Beliefs in his heart. But ultimately *Brian* is the reason that he now finds reading to be a source of long-term flourishing. *Brian* is why words on a page usher him to experience the wholeness of what the ancient Hebrews called *shalom*.

I believe that every subject area in our schools has the potential to enrich student lives long term. I'm talking about art class and physical education and science and mathematics. Social studies can do this. Performing arts classes can do this. Food and nutrition can. Agriculture science can. Computer science can do this. You've never stepped foot into a secondary course not rife with long-term flourishing potential.

In other words, schools *can* make good on their unspoken promise. They can advance the long-term flourishing of young people by leading them toward mastery in disciplines and arts that they wouldn't otherwise be likely to master. And your classes, your minutes with students? They can do this; they are wrought with this earth-shaping potential.

They *do* do this. So do mine.

You cannot convince me otherwise. I know it all the way down in the marrow of my bones. It pulses with the beating of my heart.

And what I hope, colleague, is that this book has served as a small reminder to you, too, of this truth: What you teach *matters*, and your students can be motivated to care about it because student motivation is dynamic and alive, not static and fixed. Your actions alter the cosmos because they alter human life trajectories. And I hope you'll keep reminding yourself of this until you know it with a force greater than that at the bottom of the Mariana Trench or the top of Mount Everest.

And, before we close, I want to remind you of one more thing: You and I are not the only ones who think this way, colleague. We're not even close to alone. This profession is *still* filled with smart and earnest and lovely people who *desire*—who wait on the stars—to do the work that I've been describing on every page.

One of those people is named Hannah Burnam. I met Hannah at a conference we were both attending early on in the drafting process for this book. Hannah told the story then of a student of hers, Calistra, who had called Hannah "a healer of souls." I thought that was the most beautiful little phrase to describe what a teacher does when intentionally cultivating the Five Key Beliefs.

"You may not be able to heal a body like a doctor," Calistra had told Hannah, "but there is something about you that I cannot explain."

Colleague, you and I may not be able to heal their whole lives, but we *can* become the kinds of teachers about whom students say, "There's something about you that I cannot explain." We can contemplate the reality of their souls. We can partner with their wills. We can create the conditions in which the Five Key Beliefs flourish and multiply. We can help them feel accepted and cared for and safe and connected, *not just with us but also with learning in school.*

Isn't that *something*?

Go shape the cosmos.

Teaching right beside you,

DSJR

A Special Gift

First, I really appreciate your reading the whole book. Thank you. I know there are plenty of other things you could've done instead. In teaching, there always are. As a sign of my gratitude for the time and attention you've given my book, I want to give something to you.

For a set of videos that dive deeper into this book's material, just head to davestuartjr.com/WTL-gift. This will also sign you up for my free and frequent newsletter for educators.

I love teaching, and I plan to write for teachers for as long as I'm in the classroom. I hope we can continue the conversation about how to do better, saner work, and I hope you'll be in touch with any breakthroughs in your own classroom.

About the Author

Dave Stuart Jr. is a husband and father who teaches high school in Cedar Springs, Michigan. His blog, DaveStuartJr .com, is read by over fifty thousand educators each month, and his bestselling work, *These 6 Things: How to Focus Your Teaching on What Matters Most*, has been cherished by teachers and leaders around the world. Dave is also an accomplished creator of professional development experiences and has led hundreds of impactful experiences for teachers in every U.S. state and multiple countries abroad.

Be in Touch

I speak and lead professional development for teachers all around the world. I'd love to come help equip, empower, and encourage your group with the Five Key Beliefs. You can get in touch with me very easily—just go to https://davestuartjr.com/be-in-touch and complete the simple form you find there.

Acknowledgments

In the early pages of this book, I argued that you and I are runners of a relay race in the lives of our students (see page 4); our lane is small but integral—we are necessary to make the whole complete. Without us, the finish changes.

The same can be said for this book. So many contribute to the relay race of an author's life. Authors finish work that others begin. During the long months of drafting this book, I found it impossible to comprehensively acknowledge the friends and colleagues and students and thinkers and creators who made the book in your hand. They are legion.

So, please first know that if you are reading this and you and I have met or corresponded, you blessed me; your love and earnestness helped me write this book

There are some folks I do have to name. First, thank you to my precious family. They give most for projects like this: bearing with me in my weakness, encouraging me to give me strength. Thank you to Crystal, my wife; to Hadassah, the first of our loves, who is brave and bright; to Laura Lindsay, my early partner in reading power, who is thoughtful and strong; to Marlena, the champion of wrap hugs, who is large of soul and kind of heart; to Dean, my total major guy, who is soft-hearted and observant; and to Charlie, our sweet dog.

And honor where it's due to my parents. They deserve honor. Lisa, Kathy, Sylvia; Big Dave, Brian, and Bill. Thank you.

I've had some standout mentors along the way, too: Jim Burke, who welcomed me into authorship; Brian Scriven, who welcomed me into education; Trent Gladstone, who welcomed me into divine apprenticeship; and Tim Knapp, who welcomed me into fatherhood. And I've got to shout out the leaders in my life who left the profession during the writing of this book. Being a good school leader is hard but critical. I've watched how buildings transform due to the vision and actions of single leaders. Mad respect to Ron B., Anne K., Diane W., Julie S., Carol S., and Jackie B., all of whom left leadership roles during the writing of this book.

I wrote the drafts of this book in lots of special places, such as Sweetlands Coffee in Rockford, Michigan; Cedar Springs Brewing Company; my classroom's back office (may it rest in peace); a small white cabin in Kentucky; Nick and Amber's basement; cafés in Vienna; that one coffee shop in Bishop, California; and Olivier's groovy camper in the Tucson desert. In a similar vein, thank you to the musicians: Vivaldi, Maverick City, Kate Bush, Arturo Sandoval, James Taylor, and Miles Davis.

I was going to try listing all the schools I visited during the writing of this book because I literally get new or clearer ideas on my work *every single time* I do so. But, because the book took so long to write, there are hundreds of schools and organizations that I would need to list. I do want to give a special shout-out, though, to schools that procured my services for extended professional development partnerships—looking at you Bethel, Maine; Hillsboro, Wisconsin; Linden, California; Broadalbin-Perth, New York; Oak Canyon JHS in Lindon, Utah; Tahoe City, California; and Arch Ford, Arkansas.

To my students, including those who got release forms signed to be photographed for this book: You all are a delight to be with, and I am so grateful that I got to be your teacher.

To two specific creative groups: First, Jake Knapp and John Zeratsky, who wrote *Make Time: How to Focus on What Matters Every Day* in 2018. I was having a heck of a time figuring out how to structure this book; I knew it wasn't going to be a typical Chapter 1–8 affair. And then one day it hit me: I could use the same structure these two used in their book. And second, the pyramid structure for the Five Key Beliefs was first proposed by designers at a firm called Dezudio. Each summer Dezudio works with Brooklyn Lab Charter School to turn the ideas of experts into visually communicative slides. I was invited to be part of this process when Brooklyn Lab was asking the question, "In light of all that's happened the past eighteen months, how can schools best create thriving cultures in fall 2021 and meet the unique and diverse needs of each student?" My answer, of course, was equipping educators with the Five Key Beliefs methodology.

And finally, to the Teacher: "Let me build, then, my King, a beautiful thing by long obedience, by the steady progression of long choices that laid end to end will become like the stones of a pleasing path stretching to eternity" (McKelvey, 2020).

I love that language.

May this book be a small stone on a pleasing path stretching to eternity.

References

Acho, E. (2020). *Uncomfortable conversations with a black man.* Flatiron Books.

Bishop, R. S. (1990). Mirrors, windows, and sliding glass doors. *Perspectives: Choosing and Using Books for the Classroom, 6*(3). https://scenicregional.org/wp-content/uploads/2017/08/Mirrors-Windows-and-Sliding-Glass-Doors.pdf

Brooks, A. W. (2014). Get excited: Reappraising pre-performance anxiety as excitement. *Journal of Experimental Psychology, 143*(3), 1144–1158.

Bryan, C., Yeager, D., Hinojosa, C., Chabot, A., Bergen, H., Kawamura, M., & Steubing, F. (2016). Harnessing adolescent values to motivate healthier eating. *Proceedings of the National Academy of Sciences, 113*(39), 10830–10835. https://www.pnas.org/doi/epdf/10.1073/pnas.1604586113

Clance, P. R., & Imes, S. A. (1978). The imposter phenomenon in high achieving women: Dynamics and therapeutic intervention. *Psychotherapy: Theory, Research and Practice, 15*(3), 241–247.

Clark, S., & Soutter, M. (2022). Growth mindset and intellectual risk-taking: Disentangling conflated concepts. *Phi Delta Kappan, 104*(1), 50–55.

Cohen, G. L., Garcia, J., Apfel, N., & Master, A. (2006). Reducing the racial achievement gap: A social-psychological intervention. *Science, 313,* 1307–1310.

Cohen, G. L., Garcia, J., Purdie-Vaughns, V., Apfel, N., & Brzustoski, P. (2009). Recursive processes in self-affirmation: Intervening to close the minority achievement gap. *Science, 324,* 400–403.

Collins, J. (2001). *Good to great: Why some companies make the leap and others don't.* Harper.

Coyle, D. (2018). *The culture code: The secrets of highly successful groups.* Bantam Books.

Dunlosky, J., Rawson, K. A., Marsh, E. J., Nathan, M. J., & Willingham, D. T. (2015). What works, what doesn't. *Scientific American.* https://www.scientificamerican.com/article/what-works-what-doesn-t/

Dweck, C. S. (2007). *Mindset: The new psychology of success.* Ballantine Books.

Dweck, C. S. (2018). You're not a growth mindset person (and here's why) [Video]. https://www.youtube.com/watch?v=S5Xr-8A2ziE&t=100s

Edwards, C. W. (2019). Overcoming imposter syndrome and stereotype threat: Reconceptualizing the definition of a scholar. *Taboo: The Journal of Culture and Education, 18*(1), 18–34. https://digitalcommons.lsu.edu/cgi/viewcontent.cgi?article=1205&context=taboo#:~:text=Whether%20concealing%20their%20true%20academic,avoid%20the%20perception%20of%20failure

Ericsson, A., & Pool, R. (2016). *Peak: Secrets from the new science of expertise.* Eamon Dolan/Houghton Mifflin Harcourt.

Fisher, D., Frey, N., & Smith, D. (2020). *The teacher credibility and collective efficacy playbook, grades K-12*. Corwin.

Gonzalez, J. (2015). Dogfooding: How often do you do your own assignments? *Cult of Pedagogy*. https://www.cultofpedagogy.com/dogfooding/

Gordon, D. (1999). John Wooden: First, how to put on your socks. *Newsweek*. https://www.newsweek.com/john-wooden-first-how-put-your-socks-167942

Harackiewicz, J. M., Canning, E. A., Tibbetts, Y., Priniski, S. J., & Hyde, J. S. (2016). Closing achievement gaps with a utility-value intervention disentangling race and social class. *Journal of Personal Social Psychology, 111*(5), 745–765.

Hattie, J. (2012). *Visible learning for teachers: Maximizing impact on learning*. Routledge.

Heath, C., & Starr, K. (2022). *Making numbers count: The art and science of communicating numbers*. Avid Reader Press.

Hulleman, C. S., & Harackiewicz, J. M. (2020). The utility-value intervention. In G. M. Walton & A. J. Crum (Eds.), *Handbook of wise interventions: How social psychology can help people change* (pp. 100–125). Guilford Press.

Kearney, P., Plax, T. G., Hays, L. R., & Ivey, M. J. (1991). College teacher misbehaviors: What students don't like about what teachers say or do. *Communication Quarterly, 39*, 309–324.

Koehn, D. (2001). Confucian trustworthiness and the practice of business in China. *Business Ethics Quarterly, 11*(3), 415–429. https://www.jstor.org/stable/3857847

Ladson-Billings, G. (2001). *Crossing over to Canaan: The journey of new teachers in diverse classrooms*. Josey-Bass.

Lahey, J. (2021). *The addiction innoculation: Raising healthy kids in a culture of dependence*. Harper.

Levitin, D. J. (2015). *The organized mind: Thinking straight in the age of information overload*. Plume.

Lovett, M. C. (2013). Make exams worth more than the grade: Using exam wrappers to promote metacognition. In M. Kaplan, N. Silver, D. LaVague-Manty, & D. Meizlish (Eds.), *Using reflection and metacognition to improve student learning: Across the disciplines, across the academy* (pp. 18–52). Stylus.

Marshall, K. (2022, August 15). A tribute to Bill Russell. *Marshall Memo 948*. https://www.marshallmemo.com/issue.php?I=4da4721c3cff9b18917b7d87f9e3dafc

Mason, C. (2017). *Home education*. Living Book Press.

Maya, A. (2022). Bill Walton on John Wooden. *The Orange County Register*. https://www.ocregister.com/2010/06/06/bill-walton-on-john-wooden/

McKelvey, D. (2017). *Every moment holy: Volume 1*. Rabbit Room Press.

Miu, A. S., & Yeager, D. S. (2014). Preventing symptoms of depression by teaching adolescents that people can change: Effects of a brief incremental theory of personality intervention at 9-month follow-up. *Clinical Psychological Science, 3*(5), 726–743.

Miyake, A., Kost-Smith, L. E., Finkelstein, N. D., Pollock, S. J., Cohen, G. L., & Ito, T. A. (2010). Reducing the gender achievement gap in college science: A classroom study of values affirmation. *Science, 330*, 1234–1237.

Neill, C. (2016). *Ethos: How to build credibility.* https://blog.iese.edu/speakinga saleader/ethos-how-to-build-credibility/

Pew Research Center. (2018). *Where Americans find meaning in life.* https://www .pewresearch.org/religion/2018/11/20/where-americans-find-meaning-in-life/

Pink, D. H. (2009). *Drive: The surprising truth about what motivates us.* Riverhead Books.

Piper, J. (2013). *When I don't desire God: How to fight for joy.* Crossway.

Purdie, N., & Hattie, J. (2002). Assessing students' conceptions of learning. *Australian Journal of Educational & Developmental Psychology, 2*, 17–32.

Pyne, J., & Borman, G. (2020). Replicating a scalable intervention that helps students reappraise academic and social adversity during the transition to middle school. *Journal of Research on Educational Effectiveness, 13*(4), 652–678.

Sacks, A. (2014). *Whole novels for the whole class: A student-centered approach.* Jossey-Bass.

Shree, S., & Sharma, L. (2014). The eightfold path of Buddhism for an effective & credible leadership. *SMS Varanasi.* https://www.researchgate .net/publication/324602007_The_Eightfold_Path_of_Buddhism_for_ an_Effective_Credible_Leadership

Sinek, S. (2009). *Start with why: How great leaders inspire everyone to take action.* Portfolio.

Steele, C. M., & Aronson, J. (1995). Stereotype threat and the intellectual test performance of African Americans. *Journal of Personality and Social Psychology, 69*(5), 797–811.

Strong, J. (2010). *The new Strong's expanded exhaustive concordance of the Bible* (Red letter ed.). Thomas Nelson.

Stuart, D. (2018). *These 6 things: How to focus your teaching on what matters most.* Corwin.

Telzer, E., Fuligni, A., Lieberman, M., & Galván, A. (2014). Neural sensitivity to eudaimonic and hedonic rewards differentially predict adolescent depressive symptoms over time. *Proceedings of the National Academy of Sciences of the United States of America, 111*(18), 6600–6605.

Wexler, N. (2019). *The knowledge gap: The hidden cause of America's broken education system—and how to fix it.* Avery.

Willard, D. (2002). *Renovation of the heart: Putting on the character of Christ.* NavPress.

Willingham, D. T. (2006, Spring). Knowledge in the classroom. *American Federation of Teachers.* https://www.aft.org/periodical/american-educator/ spring-2006/knowledge-classroom

Willingham, D. T. (2017). *How many people believe learning styles theories are right? And why?* http://www.danielwillingham.com/daniel-willingham-science-and-education-blog/how-many-people-believe-learning-styles-theories-are-right-and-why

Wlodkowski, R. J. (1983). *Motivational opportunities for successful teaching* [Leader's Guide]. Universal Dimensions.

Wooden, J. (2005). *On leadership: How to create a winning organization.* McGraw Hill.

Yeager, D. S., Purdie-Vaughns, V., Garcia, J., Apfel, N., Brzustoski, P., Master, A., Hessert, W. T., Williams, M. E., & Cohen, G. L. (2014). Breaking the cycle of mistrust: Wise interventions to provide critical feedback across the racial divide. *Journal of Experimental Psychology, 143*(2), 804–824.

Index

Confident Teachers, Inspired Learners

CORWIN

JONATHAN ECKERT
Focus on feedback, engagement, and well-being to support comprehensive growth while elevating the essential work of educators.

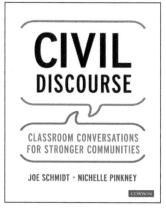

JOE SCHMIDT, NICHELLE PINKNEY
Facilitate contentious conversations by approaching civil discourse through the lenses of courage, understanding, belonging, and empathy.

CHASE NORDENGREN
Demonstrate goal setting as an integral instructional strategy to help students take ownership of their learning.

JOHN HATTIE, DOUGLAS FISHER, NANCY FREY, SHIRLEY CLARKE
Discover how working with other people can be a powerful accelerator of student learning and a precursor to future success.

To order your copies, visit **corwin.com/teachingessentials**

No matter where you are in your professional journey, Corwin books provide accessible strategies that benefit ALL learners—and ease the many demands teachers face.

CAROL PELLETIER RADFORD

Equip teachers with the tools they need to take care of themselves so they can serve their students, step into leadership, and contribute to the education profession.

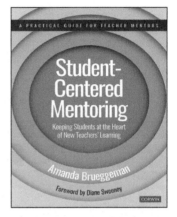

AMANDA BRUEGGEMAN

Develop student-centered approaches, promote collective efficacy, engage in coaching conversations, and prevent burnout while promoting student learning.

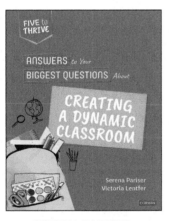

SERENA PARISER, VICTORIA LENTFER

Find actionable solutions to classroom management and culture, engaging lesson design, and effective communication.

STEPHANIE SMITH BUDHAI, KRISTINE S. LEWIS GRANT

Help teachers pivot instruction to ensure equitable, inclusive learning experiences in online and in-person settings.

A SAGE Publishing Company

Helping educators make the greatest impact

CORWIN HAS ONE MISSION: to enhance education through intentional professional learning.

We build long-term relationships with our authors, educators, clients, and associations who partner with us to develop and continuously improve the best evidence-based practices that establish and support lifelong learning.